The Drug Laws

A TIME FOR CHANGE?

BY SUSAN NEIBURG TERKEL

The Drug Laws

A TIME FOR CHANGE?

By Susan Neiburg Terkel

FRANKLIN WATTS
A Division of Grolier Publishing
New York • London • Hong Kong • Sydney
Danbury, Connecticut

This book is dedicated to my sons,
Ari and Dave Terkel

Photographs © Ari Terkel: 86 top left, 86 bottom, 106; Corbis-Bettmann: 24, 58, 86 top right; Doonesbury, 1996 G.B. Trudeau. Reprinted with permission of Universal Press Syndicate: 20; Gregory Daurer: 83, 140, 159; High Times Magazine: 108; Jamie Sheehan: 12; Jason Kapella: 152; Jim Miller: 72; Jim Roetzel: 134; The Kansas City Star: 47 (Tammy Ljungblad); Maricopa County Demand Reduction Program, 1989: 30; National Clearinghouse for Alcohol and Drug Information: 16; Reuters/Corbis-Bettmann: 67, 98, 119; Soft Secrets, Amsterdam, July 1995: 8; UPI/Corbis-Bettmann: 26, 39, 42, 52, 64, 110, 115, 122, 137, 143, 147.

Library of Congress Cataloging-in-Publication Data

Terkel, Susan Neiburg.
    The drug laws: a time for change? / by Susan Neiburg Terkel.
        p. cm. —
    Includes bibliographical references and index.
    Summary: An up-to-date study of the continuing debate over legalizing drugs, which considers legal, moral, economic, and health-related aspects of the issue.
    ISBN 0-531-11316-7
    1. Drug abuse—United States—Juvenile literature. 2. Drug legalization—United States—Juvenile literature. 3. Narcotics and crime——United States—Juvenile literature. [1. Drug abuse. 2. Drug legalization. 3. Narcotics and crime.] I. Title.
    HV5825.T47 1997
    364.1'77—DC20   96-35830
                                                                              CIP
                                                                               AC

Contents

Author's Note

This book is an inquiry, a probe, into the issue of drug legalization. I have tried to present the facts clearly, to give you all sides of the issue, so that you will be able to reach an informed decision, which may well differ from mine. This is not to say that one or both of us are right, just that we have formed our opinions using reason, which is a hallmark of a thinking person.

I would like to thank Lorna Greenberg for her astute editing. Many thanks also go to Bob Dean, Pat Jenkins, Jim Goettler, David Malmo-Levine, Mark Mauer, Monica Pratt, Jamie Sheehan, Josh Sloan, Allen St. Pierre, and my son Ari Terkel, who gave me confidence and helped me find the wonderful photos for the book.

S. N. T

A Dutch newspaper advertisement for a cannabis cafe

CHAPTER 1

Different perspectives

At the Bulldog Cafe in Amsterdam, Holland, a young crowd sips coffee. Some patrons are conversing; others are dancing to rock music pulsating through the room. In the corner, a dealer is selling marijuana and hashish, and many people in the room are openly smoking fat joints.[1] No one—not the dealer, not the patrons, not the cafe owner—is concerned about being arrested. And why should they be? It isn't going to happen.

In nearly a thousand cafes located around Amsterdam and throughout the rest of the Netherlands, the same scene occurs.[2] Although most of these cafes are privately owned, one—the Pyramid in the city of Bussum—is run by the city government. Profits from the sale of marijuana at the Pyramid help support drug education programs. Tourists in pursuit of these cafes can purchase printed guides to find them. Or they can look for little Jamaican flags posted above the door, which symbolize the small nation's liberal policy toward marijuana use.

Under the 1976 Opium Act, importing, trafficking, and possessing marijuana is illegal in the Netherlands. Yet Dutch police enforce the law selectively: they arrest suppliers of hard drugs, such as heroin, and anyone caught selling marijuana to a minor. Dutch police closed Space Cakes, a business that produced marijuana-filled baked goods. They shut down Blow Home Courier Service for delivering marijuana to customers' homes. And they closed several cafes after neighbors complained of continuous loud noise. Still, for possession, use, cultivation, and distribution of marijuana, the law bends.

In other places, the scene is different. At 7:30 A.M. on August 6, 1996, more than a hundred armed law enforcement agents stormed into the San Francisco Cannabis Buyers' Club. After breaking down the door, they seized forty thousand pounds of marijuana that was to be distributed to twelve thousand Bay Area residents, many of whom relied on marijuana to alleviate the symptoms of AIDS, cancer, and other illnesses.[3] Earlier that week, in Key West, Florida, law enforcement agents raided another of the nation's estimated thirty underground cannabis-buying clubs that distribute marijuana for medical purposes. "Police have no choice but to enforce the laws," reasoned a detective, in defense of the action. A former Key West city commissioner held a different perspective. "Where's the compassion?" he implored. "These people were dispensing medicine [marijuana] to people who can't eat, sleep, or hold food in their stomachs. The raid is nothing more than an inhumane witch hunt."

A few months later, voters in California and Arizona approved referendums to legalize the medical use of marijuana. Opponents charged that the measures were a ruse for legalizing recreational marijuana use. "A wolf dressed in sheep's clothing," the president of a national antidrug organization called them. "They're using AIDS victims and the terminally ill as props to promote the use of marijuana."[4]

According to a poll taken during the 1996 California election, only half the Californians who voted to legalize marijuana for medical use thought that it should be legal for nonmedical use. And in a national Gallup poll, fewer than 15 percent of the respondents felt that drug prohibition should end. Clearly, the contrast between Dutch and U.S. drug perspectives is stark. Throughout this book, we'll look at why U.S. drug policy is so strict and ask how well the drug laws are working.

Since marijuana is the most commonly used illicit drug and many of the people working for change are trying to change the marijuana laws, this book focuses on the controversy over legalizing marijuana. However, it is impossible to study the marijuana issue without taking a look at drug prohibition in general.

Different Perspectives

In a 1995 Gallup poll, 85 percent of the respondents opposed legalizing all drugs. During the presidential election of 1996, candidate and former senator Robert Dole advised us to say *no, no, no* to drugs. But not everyone believes that laws are the way to solve the problems caused by drug misuse or addiction. In fact, some people believe that the way drug laws are enforced creates more problems. Yet these voices of dissent differ in their perspectives and in the ways they seek change.

People are striving to achieve changes in drug laws and enforcement in diverse ways, from the voter referendums in California and Arizona to Seattle's HempFest 1995, in which fifty thousand people experienced music, pot, and speeches against prohibition. The people working for change represent a cross section, too, from conservative William F. Buckley, Jr., editor of the *National Review*, to social anarchist Stephen Gaskin of The Farm, a commune in rural Tennessee. Each sees the issue from a different perspective. What they generally agree on is that change is needed.

"Get real" approach. Some say we need to be more realistic about what the drug laws can and cannot accomplish. Limited changes are possible, but no matter how many drug laws we have, unless we become a police state, we can never stop every person from using or abusing drugs. Possible changes include: Offer needle exchange programs to intravenous (IV) drug users to stem the spread of HIV and other infectious diseases. Prescribe heroin, and perhaps cocaine, to

*The view from the stage at HempFest 95, where large crowds
gathered in support of changes in the drug laws*

addicts to curb their need to commit crimes to support drug habits.
Change laws that cannot be enforced, and so ease the burden that strict
drug laws place on the criminal justice system.

Soften the blow. Many people view our current policy as Draconian. While they favor some restrictions on drugs, such as arresting people who sell drugs to minors, they believe we ought to show more tolerance and compassion. They endorse "harm reduction"—the idea that the punishment for breaking the drug laws should not cause more harm than the drug itself.

Their recommendations include: Don't enforce the marijuana laws (de facto legalization). Change marijuana dealing from a felony (major crime) to a misdemeanor (minor crime). Make marijuana available for medical and industrial use. Offer treatment instead of punishment to nonviolent drug offenders, especially those arrested for the first time. Make treatment available to anyone who needs or wants it. Regard drug misuse and addiction as a public health issue, not a crime.

High ideals. People high on ideals—and perhaps just high—want to repeal (undo) laws against marijuana use. A few would like to end prohibitions against all drugs.

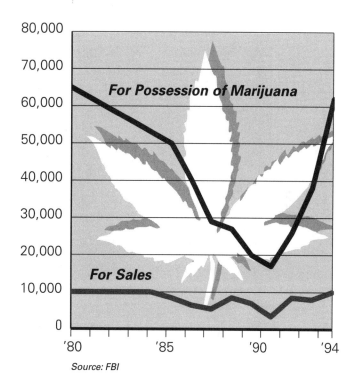

Juvenile Arrests

For Possession of Marijuana

For Sales

Source: FBI

Some of these folks claim that drugs such as marijuana and LSD are the door to creative expression, religious exaltation, social bonding, and sexual wonder. They regard experimentation with mind-altering drugs as a meaningful experience in life. Many of these people want to wear hemp, write on it, and read words printed on it, and they don't believe that other people, especially the government, have the right to stop them. In fact, they want the government to stop intruding in citizens' lives, which means no more drug testing and no more searching through cars without warrants or stopping cars displaying counterculture stickers. In short, no more invasions of privacy.

Trends in Annual Use of Drugs among Students in 1996

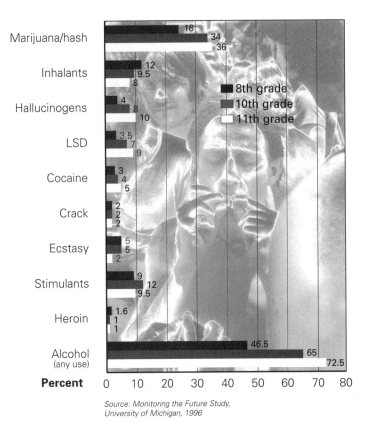

Marijuana/hash — 18, 34, 36

Inhalants — 12, 9.5, 8

Hallucinogens — 4, 8, 10

LSD — 3.5, 7, 9

Cocaine — 3, 4, 5

Crack — 2, 2, 2

Ecstasy — 5, 5, 2

Stimulants — 9, 12, 9.5

Heroin — 1.6, 1, 1

Alcohol (any use) — 46.5, 65, 72.5

Legend:
- 8th grade
- 10th grade
- 11th grade

Percent — 0 10 20 30 40 50 60 70 80

Source: Monitoring the Future Study, University of Michigan, 1996

Give up. The group embracing this approach includes many conservative people. They want to give up on prohibition and repeal the drug laws. Unlike the high idealers, this group does not sanction drug use. Instead, they want to repeal prohibition because they believe there are better ways to deal with the problems of drugs and because they believe the current drug laws create new problems.

Change course. The group promoting this approach includes many of the police chiefs in the United States who are frustrated by the results of the drug war. Instead of ending drug prohibition, they would offer drug treatment to all prisoners and anyone else who needs it. They would look for more effective ways to keep drugs out of schools, neighborhoods, jails, and prisons. And they would continue to search for more effective treatment and prevention programs.

A Common Cause

Many people seeking to improve our fight against drug abuse would like more tolerance and compassion shown those who misuse and

14

abuse drugs. They see drug use and addiction as a public health problem, not a criminal problem. Many would also like to work harder to solve the social and economic woes, such as unemployment and decaying cities, that force people to live in poverty and that promote a culture of drugs.

A large number of Americans would like to see some changes in our drug laws. Sweeping changes would obviously affect our entire society, but even small changes could have a wide impact. For example, allowing people to possess and grow small amounts of marijuana would mean several hundred thousand fewer arrests each year. A change in the ban on the sale of syringes and needles would affect the tens of thousands of people who are at risk of acquiring HIV and other infections, including the sexual partners and children of IV drug users.

Other changes could affect two million cocaine addicts and five hundred thousand heroin addicts,[5] who sometimes resort to crime in order to support their habits. Nor are the possible effects of changes to our drug policy limited to these people. Every employee subjected to drug testing, every student whose locker is sniffed by a dog trained to detect drugs, every taxpayer funding the enormous cost of the drug war—nearly $16 billion in federal expenses alone—would be affected.[6]

Let the Truth Be Told

Many people have a set attitude about drugs and our drug policy. Perhaps this was acquired through a bitter experience with alcoholism, cocaine addiction, Valium dependency, or other drug abuse. Others, especially young suburban kids experimenting with marijuana, are somewhat idealistic, in part because they are far removed from crack houses, poverty, and inner-city gangs. They smoke pot, read *High Times*, and report that a person would need to smoke forty thousand joints in fifteen minutes to overdose on weed. (If only the issue were that simple.)

Advocates of various views of the issue are all guilty of distorting information or giving incomplete accounts. For example, the American

10 Things Every Teen Should Know About Marijuana

1. Marijuana is illegal. Using, holding, buying, or selling marijuana can get you suspended, convicted of a crime, or expelled from school.

2. It's risky to your health. Marijuana is dangerous to your heart, your brain, and your lungs. It impairs motor skills like those necessary to drive a car.

3. Keep on the right track. Marijuana reduces your ability to do things that require coordination and concentration, like sports, acting, and studying.

4. You are what you wear. When you wear marijuana images on t-shirts, you are sending the *wrong* message.

5. Do the right thing. Using marijuana hurts your education, family ties, and social life.

6. Resist peer pressure. It's not easy at first, but once you establish yourself as a non-user, there will be less pressure as time goes on.

7. You don't need it. Contrary to what you might hear in songs or see on TV or in the movies, smoking marijuana does not make you cool.

8. It's not always what it seems. Marijuana can be laced with crack cocaine or PCP without you even knowing it.

9. Talk about your problems. Using marijuana won't help you escape your problems, it will only create more. Don't believe people who say that marijuana is no big deal, or that it will make your life better.

10. Everybody's NOT doing it. Over 86 percent of 12- to 17-year-olds have never even tried marijuana. Marijuana won't make you happy or popular or help you learn the skills you need as you grow up. You can do that with the help of friends, family, and other adults you trust.

The U.S. governmental policy toward drug use is quite clear: Zero tolerance of drugs, including marijuana.

Medical Association (AMA) has neither endorsed nor condemned the medical use of marijuana, but opponents of marijuana imply that the AMA has condemned the idea. Similarly, marijuana supporters point out that no one dies from using marijuana, but some people have died in accidents after using marijuana—accidents that might have been prevented if they had not been spaced out.

Unless we are absolutely truthful, any discussion of the issue becomes an exercise in sophistry (faulty reasoning). It is essential, therefore, to use clarity, and not emotion, to look at a few of the controversies.

Marijuana is a gateway drug. It is true that many people who abuse alcohol, shoot heroin, and get hooked on cocaine began their journey into hard drugs by smoking a joint. But it is also usually true that people willing to take risks take all kinds of risks. A teenager likely to engage in premarital or unprotected sex is also more likely to drink, smoke, and do drugs. Yet, one behavior does not necessarily *cause* another behavior.

Nor do most people using marijuana go on to harder drugs. After all, nearly eighty million Americans have tried marijuana, yet fewer than three million are addicted to cocaine or heroin. (Three million addicts, however, is definitely cause for concern.) As with drinking, many people can smoke marijuana, albeit in defiance of the law, without ruining their lives. Still, far too many people cannot, and they deserve a drug policy that takes them into consideration, not because of the problems they have and create, but because they are, after all, members of our society.

Marijuana is not harmless. Compared to other drugs, including legal ones such as alcohol, tobacco, and caffeine, marijuana is relatively harmless *physically*. For individuals susceptible to high blood pressure, however, marijuana can be harmful. And, as with cigarettes, long-term smoking can damage a person's lungs. Further, some researchers believe that in males, marijuana inhibits the production of testosterone, which can decrease the sperm count and cause a delay in puberty.

Because marijuana alters a person's depth perception and sense of

Percentage of Students Who Have Tried Marijuana, Cigarettes, or Alcohol

■ 8th grade ■ 10th grade ☐ 12th grade

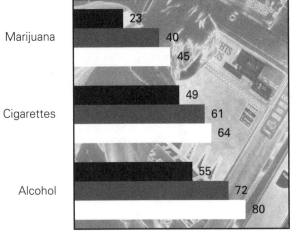

Marijuana
23
40
45

Cigarettes
49
61
64

Alcohol
55
72
80

Percent 0 10 20 30 40 50 60 70 80 90 100

Source: Monitoring the Future Study,
University of Michigan, 1996

time, it can slow down physical reactions and decrease the ability to make careful decisions. Stephen Gaskin, a supporter of marijuana legalization, says he believes that teenagers ought to wait until they "take up as much space as a grownup, eat as much food as a grownup, and work as much as a grownup" before using marijuana. In his article "Cannabis Spirituality," published in *High Times*, he advises students to refrain from using marijuana (this is not Officer Friendly speaking; this is an old hippie who believes that adults have the right to use marijuana): "When children get an early introduction to cannabis, too often they go immediately to the limits of habituation and supply. It becomes something that structures their time, and they neglect their education." Gaskin adds this advice: "Kids don't need any extraneous things standing between them and learning their life tools. Sometimes cannabis puts kids on ego trips . . . makes them think they are already grown up and they don't need to try."[7]

While it is difficult to make a case that marijuana causes reefer madness (crazed behavior the government once attributed to the drug), in individuals prone to mental illness, marijuana can cause paranoia. It may also hasten the onset of manic depression and schizophrenia in individuals at risk.

Today's marijuana may be more dangerous to use than the marijuana people smoked in the 1960s and 1970s. Marijuana potency is

18

measured by its THC content (the psychoactive component of marijuana). In 1968, the government began measuring the potency of confiscated marijuana and determined that the THC content was between 1 and 3 percent. However, storing the samples improperly or too long could affect the THC content. Further, small samples might not represent what was really on the market.

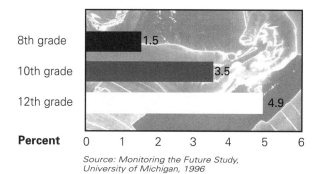

Daily Use of Marijuana among Students, 1996 Study

8th grade — 1.5
10th grade — 3.5
12th grade — 4.9

Percent   0   1   2   3   4   5   6

Source: Monitoring the Future Study, University of Michigan, 1996

Although some very expensive marijuana has a high THC content, today's marijuana *averages* between 3 and 4 percent THC, based on samples analyzed by the government's Potency Monitoring Program and reported in its 1994 quarterly report.[8] Even if earlier THC levels were less than 3 percent, this increase hardly justifies claims of ten- or forty-fold increases made by those opposed to marijuana use.

More young people today are smoking marijuana, whatever the THC content, that has been tainted with other drugs. Blunts are cigars that have been refilled with marijuana. Occasionally, PCP or cocaine is added to the marijuana, and that addition may be detectable only after the blunt has been smoked.

If it's good enough for you, it's good enough for me. In an atmosphere in which the fear of drug use prevails, parents who grew up during the 1960s and 1970s are skittish about admitting to their own drug use (especially if they never quit). Most merely tell their children not to use marijuana. After years of "just saying no to drugs," however, more and more young people are saying *yes*, especially to marijuana. In 1995, one in three high school seniors, one in four sophomores, and one in six eighth graders—and probably nine in ten students reading

this book—used marijuana.[9] And the trend suggests that many more young people will be joining those ranks.

In a magazine editorial, *Doonesbury* cartoonist Garry Trudeau suggested that it is time for these parents to fess up. He believes that those who used marijuana should admit they did and be honest about the experience.[10]

However, this is not going to be a book about using drugs per se. For whether we repeal every drug law or restrict drug use even more, all people—teens and adults alike—must learn to make intelligent choices about drugs, including those that are legal.

Complicated problems take time to resolve and drug use, abuse, and prohibition are all complicated issues. Still, some people are looking at the issue of marijuana and other drug prohibition and asking: Is it time for a change?

CHAPTER 2

Guardians among Us

In 1988, scientists discovered a protein receptor in the brain for THC (tetrahydrocannabinol—the psychoactive ingredient in marijuana) in a region where higher learning takes place. Evidence of this protein on the surface of brain cells suggests that the brain makes a natural substance that resembles marijuana and affects mood and memory in a similar way.[1] "It's not just an accident that they [THC and the receptor] fit," explained one of the discoverers. "The body makes these receptors to accept chemicals that are important."[2]

Our bodies produce chemicals that are found elsewhere in nature. For example, our brains can make opiates, called enkephalins, which relieve pain and anxiety.[3] Similarly, we know that when people become infatuated, their brains manufacture amphetamines, which cause the euphoria of love, including lovers' ability to stay awake an exceptionally long time.[4]

Some scientists suggest that since people are chemical organisms, it is natural for them to react to the chemistry around them. One scientist, Ronald Siegel, has tried to prove this through research in the behavior of animals. According to Siegel, many insects and animals use chemicals, from the California robins that get high on Pryancatha berries to Australia's cuddly koala bears, who eat eucalyptus leaves.[5] During the Vietnam War, water buffalo were observed nibbling more opium poppy than usual, perhaps, suggests Siegel, in response to the noise and disruption of the war—much the way many U.S. soldiers were using marijuana and heroin to ease their stress.

The Danger of Smoking

For every three teenagers who begins smoking today, one will die a tobacco-related death. Five million Americans under age 18 will die tobacco-related deaths

Source: New York Times editorial, October 24, 1995

Some people fail to use drugs appropriately or safely. Tobacco, alcohol, and caffeine, all of which are legal, erode the health of thousands of Americans each year. Excessive consumption of alcohol causes a third of all deaths and injuries from car accidents, is associated with most of the rapes (90 percent) that occur on college campuses,[6] and during pregnancy causes fetal alcohol syndrome. Nor is tobacco less harmful. Tobacco will cause the premature death of five million teenagers smoking today. This year alone, more than four hundred thousand people will die because they smoked, and many more will suffer from cancer, lung disease, and other ailments.[7]

In the Course of History

Our cultural history demonstrates a strong reliance on drugs. Alcohol is part of many Western religious ceremonies. Many settlers considered alcohol a harmless beverage for their children, and the economy of the South thrived on tobacco cultivation.

For centuries, drugs such as marijuana and opium were used to treat illnesses, especially when little was known about the causes of disease. Compared to other remedies of the 1700s and 1800s—such as bloodletting, purging, and leeching—opiates were extraordinarily effective for treatment of a multitude of symptoms, such as pain, sleeplessness, anxiety, diarrhea, and coughing. Besides relieving physical symptoms, opiates gave patients a euphoric respite.

With the invention of the syringe in 1856, caretakers could inject a drug directly into a muscle or vein, giving patients swift relief. By 1881, as medical historian David T. Courtwright notes, "A syringe of morphine, in a very real sense, was a magic wand. It could cure little, but it could relieve anything. . . . Doctors and patients alike were tempted to overuse it."[8]

Heroin was first marketed in 1898 by a German pharmaceutical firm, the Bayer Company (which also held the patent on aspirin). Like morphine, heroin was touted as a miracle drug, with no side effects. Medically, it was used to treat respiratory ailments and was effective, no doubt, because it relaxed sufferers.

In general, narcotics were widely available and used. Patients could get them from their doctors or buy them as home remedies, which were sold by mail, over the counter, and by door-to-door peddlers. Mothers gave their crying babies "soothing formulas" laced with opium and heroin.

In the following years, however, much was learned about the origins of disease and illness. The "germ theory" gained acceptance, and less addictive drugs were discovered for medical use. For many people, most of whom were law-abiding citizens, these discoveries came too late to prevent their addiction to the narcotics they had used for medical problems.

Throughout our history, narcotics and other drugs have also been used for nonmedical purposes. Coca-Cola's original formula, like that of similar beverages of the day, contained a significant amount of cocaine. It was even advertised as a nonalcoholic "temperance" drink. In 1903 the company switched to caffeine, a less harmful, but nonetheless addictive, drug.

Many laborers relied on cocaine to give them strength and endurance.

A New York opium den, in 1925

Explained one hard-working cargo handler: "I can work up to seventy hours at a stretch without sleep or rest, in rain, in cold, and in heat."[9]

Opium smoking, which was introduced into the United States by Chinese immigrants during the mid-1800s, grew in popularity, especially among the fringe members of society—gamblers, thieves, and prostitutes—and certain members of the upper-class avant-garde.

Since the colonial period, the hemp plant (another name for marijuana, a plant native to Asia) has been a major crop in the United States, used to make paper, rope, and cloth, as well as to treat medical conditions. Its use for recreational purposes began around 1910 with the Mexican immigrants who used it to achieve euphoria. Its acceptance also grew among Southern blacks, jazz and blues musicians, and others in the arts. (Only later, during the Vietnam War years, did its use spread widely among soldiers, students, and others.)

Although it is difficult to be accurate about the number of drug addicts in the United States, when the idea of drug prohibition took root there were probably between two hundred thousand and four hundred thousand.[10] Then, mounting pressure to do something about this problem led Congress to pass the Pure Food and Drug Act in 1906. The law required that all active ingredients, especially cocaine, opium, and other addictive drugs, be noted on a product's label. Thus began the quest to regulate drugs and prevent drug abuse.

The politics of Drugs

By 1909, many U.S. businesses wanted to trade with China, which had a serious opium problem. An estimated ninety million Chinese citizens had an addiction to opium. From the time it acquired the Philippine Islands in 1898, the U.S. had its own narcotics problem. To address drug addiction in China and other territories, an international conference was held in Shanghai, China, in 1909.

Two years later, a second conference took place in The Hague, Netherlands, and an international accord was reached. In the treaty, the Hague Convention of 1912, thirty-four participating nations agreed to

25

A 1919 photograph shows kegs of bootleg (illegally produced) beer being dumped into Lake Michigan. The government repealed alcohol prohibition in 1934 but, despite its failure, began the prohibition of marijuana in 1937.

control narcotics. The use of opium was to be limited to the practice of medicine. Other uses, such as recreational smoking, were condemned. To control the narcotics trade, each nation agreed to set a quota on how much it would import or export, a quota limited to medical purposes.

The United States was now in an embarrassing situation. The idea of international control of narcotics had come from the American delegation. Yet on U.S. soil, there was little control. Indeed, opium imports were legal and had produced nearly twenty-seven million dollars in tax revenues over the years. To deal with the situation, the U.S. delegates to the Hague Conference convinced Congress to pass a law restricting the sale of opium and cocaine. Thus, on December 17, 1914, the Harrison Act, named for Representative Francis Burton Harrison, the Democrat who ushered the bill through Congress, became law. The act allowed small quantities of opium and cocaine to be sold over the counter. Larger amounts could be prescribed by doctors or dentists, who were required to record the transactions with a central agency. Anyone who manufactured or dispensed drugs was subject to regulation.

When the Harrison Act went into effect many physicians continued to prescribe drugs to patients who were addicts. Pharmacists continued to fill those prescriptions. Some physicians and pharmacists did so out of compassion. Others, called "dope doctors," prescribed drugs for anyone who wanted them, sometimes for hundreds of people a day. In addition, a black market run by dealers eager to exploit the demand for drugs emerged. The difficulty of securing a legal supply of drugs drove prices up. This led some drug users to resort to crime to pay those prices.

Originally, the Harrison Act was meant to regulate the sale of narcotics; it was not intended to ban them. Ultimately, however, it banned all but medical drug use. How did a law meant to regulate drugs wind up prohibiting them? After World War I, there was fear that drug use would harm the nation's ability to defend itself militarily in case of another war. Added to this was the popular notion that all drug use, including alcohol use, was a sign of moral weakness—a sin. The temperance movement, a strong movement against alcohol consumption, had pushed through the passage of the Eighteenth Amendment in 1919, prohibiting the sale or consumption of alcohol. The newer perception that drug addiction was a sin and a crime, and no longer an illness or a social problem, led to a reinterpretation of the Harrison Act.

In 1919, the issue of drug abuse was put to the Supreme Court in the case of *Webb et al. v. The United States*. Based on a single clause in the Harrison Act—that drugs could be legally dispensed only in the course of professional practice[11]—the Court decided that professional practice excluded giving drugs to people just to maintain their drug habits. "It is so plain a perversion of meaning," the justices wrote, "that no discussion of the subject is required."[12]

Reinterpretation of the Harrison Act denied addicts any legal source of drugs. Physicians and pharmacists who continued to supply them were subject to arrest. Indeed, after the *Webb et al.* decision, hundreds of physicians and pharmacists were arrested.

A few years later, in 1925, the Court declared addiction to be a medical, not a criminal, matter, a position reaffirmed in 1962. While it was not a crime to *be* an addict, it was (and still is) illegal for an addict or anyone else to *use* illicit drugs. Soon, many Americans regarded marijuana use as criminal, an act to be punished by long prison sentences and high fines.

In 1937, a government regulatory agency called the Narcotics Bureau issued a report warning that marijuana use leads to "general instability, mental weakness, and finally insanity . . . and is turning Americans into monsters. . . . A malicious madman is being created."[13] To educate Americans about the dangers of marijuana, the federal government produced *Reefer Madness,* a film that dramatized—and to its critics, overdramatized—the effects of marijuana use. More notable, however, was the passage of the 1937 Marijuana Tax Act, which placed a one-hundred-dollar-per-ounce tax on the nonindustrial use of hemp, along with a stiff prison sentence for anyone who evaded the tax.

Since the 1914 Harrison Act, which was later amended to include a ban on heroin, and the 1937 Marijuana Tax Act, dozens of state and federal laws prohibiting drug use have been enacted. In 1970, the federal laws were combined into a single, comprehensive law, called the Controlled Substance Act (CSA), which remains in effect.

Waging War on Drugs

During the 1960s, illicit drug use increased dramatically. At least half the American soldiers who served in the Vietnam War used drugs, especially heroin and marijuana. When they returned, one out of five was chemically dependent. Although most of these veterans managed to rid themselves of their addiction, the situation so alarmed the U.S. military that they initiated drug testing in 1971.

Drug use also increased alarmingly among the nation's youth. By 1969, twenty-four million Americans had tried marijuana and other illicit drugs. In 1971, President Richard Nixon responded to this crisis with a declaration of war on drugs. He established the Commission on Marijuana and Drug Abuse to research the problem and report back to Congress with recommendations for a national policy to stem the use of illegal drugs.

After two years of research and evaluation, the commission presented a report with several recommendations, including that marijuana be decriminalized. This meant that possession of small amounts of marijuana would result in a fine, not a prison sentence. Nixon ignored the report and announced the nation had turned the corner in the battle.

The next two administrations—Gerald Ford's and Jimmy Carter's—adopted more tolerant drug policies. President Carter even suggested adopting the commission's recommendation to decriminalize marijuana. Between 1973 and 1979, this is precisely what eleven states—Oregon, Alaska, Maine, Colorado, California, Ohio, Minnesota, Mississippi, North Carolina, New York, and Nebraska—did. (In 1990, Alaska reversed the decision.)

By the 1980s, however, the issue of drug use reemerged as a paramount national concern. This was due partly to the drug deaths of several famous people, including basketball star Len Bias and comedian John Belushi. The dangerous new drug epidemic of crack cocaine and the situation in Latin America, where drug kingpins reigned, scared the American public into accelerating the drug war. In addition, the spread of HIV infection among drug users heightened public panic and resolve.

Responding to the rising alarm, in 1989 President George Bush spearheaded a commitment to "zero tolerance." Bush appointed William Bennett to head the new Office of National Drug Control Policy and lead the nation's war on drugs, dubbing Bennett "the drug czar." Bennett's first report to Congress stated that the U.S. could win the war on drugs only by stepping up its efforts and expenditures. Enthusiastically (and perhaps naively), Bennett predicted that in the next decade drug use could be cut in half.

In many areas, current drug enforcement policy can be summed up as Do Drugs. Do Time.

By the time Bennett was replaced with Clinton administration appointee Lee Brown, a former police chief, the drug czar had become a presidential cabinet secretary. This change helped Brown coordinate the efforts of the different federal agencies—the DEA (Drug Enforcement Agency, a federal agency in the Justice Department), the FBI, U.S. Customs, the Coast Guard, and others—engaged in the drug war. Both Brown and his successor, retired general Barry McCaffrey, put aside the analogy to war. Instead they saw the issue as a monumental problem. "You cannot succeed in this effort," explained Brown at a town meeting, "by declaring war on our citizens."[14]

During President Bill Clinton's first term in office, marijuana use among teenagers rose sharply. As he campaigned for a second term, his opponent, Bob Dole, strongly criticized him for being soft on drugs. Marijuana use had risen dramatically in three years, and the use of heroin, LSD, and other drugs was on the rise, as well. Drug crime violence, though down, remained a scourge in the cities, and many foreign nations remained havens for drug kingpins.

Still, Clinton hardly deserved the accusation of being soft on drugs. During his first term, more money was spent enforcing drug laws than ever before. Three times as many people were arrested—1.5 million—on drug charges than during the previous administration. The nation's jails and prisons held a record number of nonviolent drug offenders. And the sentences meted out for marijuana, cocaine, and amphetamine possession were, in some cases, lengthier than those for many rapists, burglars, and child abusers.

Changing the Laws

There are several possible ways to change the laws that have been passed since drug prohibition began. These include:

Legalization. In one version of this model, all of the drug laws would be repealed or changed. The United States would revert to its pre-Harrison Act drug policy.

A more moderate approach would be to repeal some of the laws, such as the 1937 Marijuana Tax Act. This would allow society to retain laws against manufacturing, selling, or using highly addictive drugs, known as "hard drugs."

Government regulation. In this approach to drug law reform, certain drugs that are not now legally available, such as heroin and marijuana, would be made available, perhaps in government-run clinics. Drugs would be treated as medications instead of as criminal substances. Thus, people addicted to a drug like heroin could receive a government supply of the drug instead of having to buy it (or steal for it) from dealers connected to organized crime and gangs, or from other dangerous people.

De facto legalization. With this approach, certain drug laws are not enforced. Accordingly, people who break those laws are not arrested or penalized for the violation. De facto legalization allows society to treat the problems of addiction and drug misuse without putting nonviolent drug offenders in jail.

Decriminalization. A few states have decriminalized marijuana possession. This means that someone can be arrested for possession of a small amount of marijuana, but the crime is a misdemeanor, not a felony. Defendants are tried in civil, rather than criminal courts.

Anyone arrested for possession of a small amount of marijuana in New Hampshire, which decriminalized marijuana possession, is fined one thousand dollars. In contrast, anyone arrested for possessing the same amount of marijuana in Michigan—a strict drug law state—faces a one-year prison term and a ten-thousand-dollar fine.

For nearly a century, U.S. lawmakers have concerned themselves with the issue of drug use and abuse. During this time, they have enacted more and more laws—and more and more Americans have broken those laws. As we enter the next century—and the next millennium—some Americans are saying: Isn't it time for a change?

CHAPTER 3

Are the Drug Laws Too Harsh?

Charisse was a high school senior in Alabama when she fell in love with Jeff, a small-time local dealer who sold LSD and Ecstasy. On a few occasions Charisse accompanied Jeff while he made a drug deal. When Jeff was busted for drug dealing, Charisse was arrested too, even though she had no drugs in her possession and had never sold drugs. Charisse was charged with conspiracy to deal drugs, and she received the minimum sentence required by law—ten years in prison with no chance of parole. The sentencing judge said that he regretted having to mete out such a harsh sentence to a first-time, nonviolent offender. But the law allowed him no alternative.

A student at the University of Virginia was caught selling three-quarters of an ounce of marijuana and a bag of hallucinogenic mushrooms.[1] For drug trafficking, he was sentenced to over a year in federal prison with no possibility of parole. The judge lamented that he could not order a less severe sentence, considering the student's good academic record and previously clean slate. "It tears up the court's conscience in a case like this," admitted the judge, "but if I am to be true to my oath, I have no choice but to follow federal directives."[2] Most people using an illicit drug know that they are breaking the law. And as the adage says: Don't do the crime if you can't do the time. Nevertheless, many people fail to comprehend the seriousness of the drug laws or the severity of the penalties for breaking them.

Consider these two cases: For helping to unload hashish from a boat, first-time offender Michael T. was sentenced to eight years in federal prison. For renting a truck for a friend to import marijuana, first-time offender Charles D. also received an eight-year sentence.[3]

The question many drug law reformers ask is not whether drugs are harmful, for most people agree that heroin, crack, PCP, and other drugs are extremely dangerous. Instead, they pose the question that President Jimmy Carter asked during his term in office: Do drug *laws* do more harm than the drugs themselves do? They also ask if it is right for a society to enact and enforce laws that so many citizens defy.

As Drug Laws Now Stand

The purpose of the federal government's Controlled Substance Act (CSA) is to ensure that drugs regarded as dangerous are used only for medical purposes, and that when they are used, they are used safely.

Not all drugs are regulated by the CSA. Natural and chemically derived substances, such as San Padre cactus, morning glory seeds, and nutmeg, for example, are legal when used for normal gardening, cooking, or decorative purposes. Yet according to Adam Gottlieb, author of *Legal Highs*, these substances can produce an intense psychedelic experience if ingested in large enough quantities.

Other drugs are not prohibited but are regulated. Cigarettes, for instance, may not be advertised on television, sold to minors, or smoked in most public buildings.

Finally, drugs like antibiotics require a prescription but avoid regulation by the CSA, which supervises only drugs considered addictive

Penalties for Breaking Drug Laws

SCHEDULE	FIRST OFFENSE		SUBSEQUENT OFFENSES	
	Prison Sentence	*Max. Fine*	*Prison Sentence*	*Max. Fine*
I & II	0-20 yrs.	$1 million	0-30 yrs.	$2 million
III	0-5 yrs.	$250,000.	0-10 yrs.	$500,000
IV	0-3 yrs.	$250,000.	0-6 yrs.	$500,000
V	0-1 yr.	$100,000	0-2 yrs.	$200,000

Source: U.S. Dept. of Justice

or widely abused—namely narcotics, cannabis, stimulants, amphetamines, and hallucinogens.

Depending on a drug's purported danger, it is classified into one of five categories, or "schedules."

Schedule I is the most restrictive. Drugs in this category, such as LSD, heroin, and marijuana, are judged highly addictive, dangerous, and without any accepted medical use. They are allowed only for strictly supervised medical experimentation.

Schedule II drugs, such as cocaine and morphine, are also highly restricted and require a doctor's prescription.

Schedule III drugs (Tylenol with codeine and some barbiturates), schedule IV drugs (Valium and other tranquilizers), and schedule V drugs (over-the-counter cough medicines) are monitored and regulated. Some are sold over the counter; others require the patient's signature and records are kept of the sale.

If new information suggests that a drug is more or less dangerous than was believed, its schedule can be changed. For example, years ago, amphetamines did not require a prescription. When nonmedical amphetamine use spread, it was rescheduled to a stricter category that requires a prescription.

Criteria for Regulating Drugs

Schedule	Potential for Abuse	Medical Use	Safety or Dependence Physical-Psychological
I	great	only experimental or safety unknown	regarded as unsafe
II	great	yes	high chance of physical and psychological dependence
III	moderate	yes	moderate or low chance of physical dependence/high chance of psychological dependence
IV	low	yes	limited dependence/less than Schedule III drugs
V	low	yes	limited/less chance of dependence than Schedule IV drugs

Scheduling Drugs

Three criteria are used to judge each drug and determine if or how it should be scheduled. The criteria are as follows:

Medical use. Because most hallucinogens have no *recognized* medical use, they are categorized as Schedule I, highly restricted drugs. Heroin is also a Schedule I drug because its medical use is considered obsolete now that newer, less addictive, pain relievers are available. (Heroin is still used to relieve pain in hospice programs treating terminally ill patients outside the United States.)

Potential for abuse. Another criterion for regulating drugs is their "potential for abuse," which refers to how people tend to use a particular drug. For example, anabolic steroids used to require prescriptions but were not scheduled drugs. Due to widespread nonmedical use among athletes and bodybuilders, the federal government scheduled anabolic steroids. They may be prescribed for medical use, but since they are now a scheduled drug, supplying them for nonmedical use is a crime and subject to a stiff penalty.

Safety. If a drug leads to bizarre behavior, hallucinations, or other unpredictable effects that threaten the safety of the user or others, it will be strictly scheduled.

Dependence liability. Will users suffer withdrawal symptoms, such as nausea and chills, if they stop taking the drug? Will they crave a drug, such as cocaine, and believe they have to have it, even though they have few or no physical symptoms? If users can become physically or psychologically addicted to a drug, it will be scheduled.

Anyone handling scheduled drugs, such as hospital or pharmacy staff, must be registered with the Drug Enforcement Agency (DEA). They are required to keep sales records and inventory accounts of all scheduled drugs. This may be as simple as keeping a list of signatures of those who purchase a Schedule V drug, or as complicated as filling out numerous forms when prescribing a Schedule I drug in research. The CSA sets standards for storing scheduled drugs, especially Schedule I and II drugs, which must be kept in vaults or burglar-proof safes.

In the Name of the Law

When Adam B. stood next to his souped-up car and handed a friend a pack of cigarettes, a police officer construed the behavior as a drug deal and searched Adam's car. When he found an ounce of marijuana in Adam's backpack, he arrested him.

As the marijuana was packaged in four separate bags, the judge at Adam's trial determined that he had intended to sell it. Adam was charged with possession of marijuana with intent to sell, a charge that carries a far stiffer penalty than mere possession.

Like Adam, most people know when they are breaking a drug law.

Average Length of Sentence Imposed for Drug Trafficking

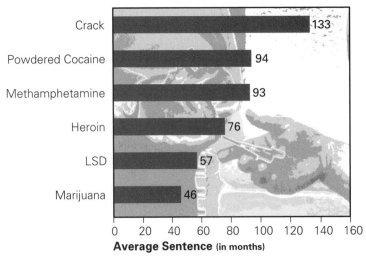

Drug	Average Sentence (in months)
Crack	133
Powdered Cocaine	94
Methamphetamine	93
Heroin	76
LSD	57
Marijuana	46

Average Sentence (in months)

Source: Bureau of Justice Statistics, 1994

Many, however, are unaware of the price they may pay if caught and convicted—until compelled to pay that price. And that price can be quite high.

One man knew he was committing a crime when he purchased 300 pounds (136 kg) of marijuana for his own use and to sell to friends. Someone informed on him, and he was arrested. Although his wife had never smoked marijuana, she was also arrested—and sentenced to five years in prison because she was aware of her husband's activities.

Neither the severity of the penalties nor the government's campaign to educate people about the danger of drugs has stopped drug use or abuse. (Laws against murder, rape, and child abuse don't stop those crimes, either.) On the other hand, better enforcement of the drug laws has led to a drop in homicide and violent crime in certain places. Still, if a person convicted of growing marijuana plants can serve more time than someone convicted of rape,[4] and if possessing or selling 650 grams of cocaine or heroin in Michigan, even if it is a first-time offense, can bring a sentence of life in prison with no chance of parole, the drug laws seem unfair to many, and the penalties too harsh.

Laws are a society's prescription for a good and decent life. They are supposed to keep society's members from harming each other, and to punish those who inflict harm. It is neither impossible nor desirable to enact enough laws to govern all of human behavior. Nor would most of us choose to live in a society in which every single act is regulated.

A scene at a treatment center for teens. Treatment has been shown to be seven times more effective than enforcement and interdiction in reducing the number of people who use cocaine.

Besides, we have a pluralistic society, in which members hold different and sometimes opposing viewpoints. On tough issues like abortion, capital punishment, and gun control the justice system cannot accommodate everyone's viewpoints, or even find a middle ground on certain issues. To understand our justice system more clearly, Vincent Bugliosi, a former prosecutor,[5] offers this lesson: The law has two classifications of crime, and the difference between the two is essential.

Malum in se (a wrong in itself). This is a crime resulting from morally reprehensible behavior. Examples are rape, murder, and theft. Such behavior has been wrong through all time. Fortunately, a small percentage of the population—less than 1 percent in the U.S.—commit such crimes.

Many people who commit crimes of *malum in se* are using a drug such as cocaine, amphetamines, or alcohol. Some are acting as members of a major drug-dealing organization or they are stealing money to support a drug habit.

Malum prohibition (a wrong forbidden by law). This is a crime because it involves behavior that is against the law, but not necessarily considered evil. Some people argue that drug use is sinful, just as the temperance societies fighting for alcohol prohibition viewed drinking as evil. Nearly 80 million U.S. citizens—one out of three adults—have committed a crime of *malum prohibition* by smoking marijuana.

Drug laws are supposed to protect people from themselves and keep them from harming others. Because the drug laws raise the price of drugs, and thus users, especially addicts, may resort to thefts, burglaries, robberies, and other crimes of *malum in se*, critics of the drug laws question their value.

Getting Tough on Crime

Mandatory Sentencing

To get "tough on crime," federal lawmakers designed a program of mandatory sentencing, giving uniformity to drug crime penalties. No guesswork. No leniency. And no mercy in minimum sentencing.

Mandatory sentencing was first tried in 1951, when Congress passed the Boggs Act. By 1970, the resulting severe prison overcrowding and judges' loss of discretion in sentencing led to its repeal.

Then, in 1986, the crack epidemic began capturing daily headlines. It was an election year, and many politicians were eager to respond to the crack epidemic and to appear tough on drugs and crime. They ignored the reasons why mandatory minimum sentencing had been repealed, enacted the toughest crime bill ever, and reestablished mandatory minimum sentencing.

The repercussions ripped through both the crime world and the judicial system. Once again, the nation's jails and prisons experienced

Federal Mandatory Drug Sentences

Type of Drug	5-Year Sentence without Parole	10- Year Sentence without Parole
LSD	1 gram	10 grams
Marijuana	100 plants or 100 kilos	1000 plants or 1000 kilos
Crack Cocaine	5 grams	50 grams
Powder Cocaine	500 grams	5 kilos
Heroine	100 grams	1 kilo
Methamphetamine	10 grams	100 grams
PCP	10 grams	100 grams

serious overcrowding. Once again, many judges regretted the lack of discretion and flexibility in sentencing drug offenders.

Michael R., age twenty-two, sold a rock of crack cocaine that weighed 5.257 grams—less than the weight of three dimes—to an undercover police officer for twenty dollars. Since Michael had no previous criminal record and seemed unlikely to repeat the crime, the judge wished to put him on probation. This would punish him but keep him out of jail, where exposure to hardened criminals and drug dealers, plus easy access to drugs, would be detrimental to him, and therefore to society as well. But because of the state's mandatory minimum sentencing requirement, the judge was compelled to sentence him to five years in prison.

Sentence cliffs. Another problem with rigid sentencing procedures is the "sentencing cliff." A person charged with possession of 4.99 grams of crack gets a sentence of one year in jail. In contrast, someone charged with possession of 5.01 grams—only .02 grams more, an

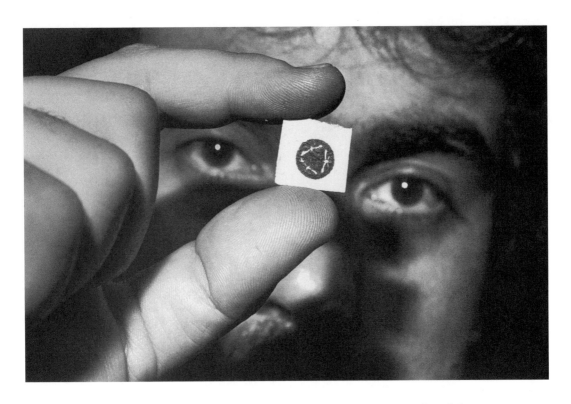

*A person selling LSD can be charged with the weight of the
LSD plus the weight of the material the drug is on.*

amount weighing less than a feather—will receive a five-year prison sentence.

In defense of the law, a person has a choice not to possess or sell *any* amount of crack. At the same time, one of the basic principles of the Constitution and the Bill of Rights is the protection of citizens from unreasonable punishment. Sentence cliffs undermine that principle.

Critics cite other flaws in our drug crime sentences. For one, the charge always includes the weight of the material on which a drug is sold in addition to the actual drug. A person selling LSD is charged with the weight of the LSD plus the weight of the paper it is on. The weight of the paper can lead to many more years in prison. A person may also be charged for the entire weight of a marijuana plant—even though only a part of it is smokable or ingestible.

Another disparity in sentencing exists in relation to crack cocaine and powder cocaine. For a person convicted of possessing 500 grams of cocaine or 5 grams of crack cocaine—same substance, different form—the sentence will be a prison term of five years.

Critics of the policy believe that it is unfair. They also believe that it is racist, since poor black Americans are more likely to use crack cocaine, the cheaper drug, rather than powder cocaine. Eighty percent of the cocaine consumed in the U.S. is taken by white people. Yet in 1994, 90 percent of those convicted of Federal crack offenses were black. And a crack offense carries substantially harsher sentences. In 1996, the issue was put before the Supreme Court and the policy upheld. The discrepancy—and critics would argue, the racism—persists.

Three srikes and you're out. Criminologists have learned that most (70 percent) of the violent crime in the United States is committed by a core group of people who have committed previous crimes. To keep these repeat rapists, muggers, and murderers from committing more crimes, more than thirty states now have three-strikes-and-you're-out mandatory life sentencing. Any person convicted of a third felony—a violent crime or a serious drug crime (growing a thousand marijuana plants is considered a serious drug crime)—will be sentenced to life imprisonment with no chance of parole.

Mark Y. was convicted of two drug offenses in his early twenties. In the first crime, he had used a false prescription to purchase a drug for someone else. In the second, he was charged with possession of quaaludes. Twenty years later, Mark was convicted of a third crime— conspiracy to distribute marijuana.[6] All three of his crimes were non-violent, yet because of his state's three-strikes-and-you're-out policy, Mark received life imprisonment.

For crimes of *malum in se*, such as assault, rape, child molestation, or certain cases of manslaughter (such as those involving repeated drunk driving), the policy of three strikes and you're out may be justifiable. For nonviolent crimes such as most drug crimes—possessing marijuana and selling small amounts of it—critics condemn the policy as too harsh and a frivolous use of taxpayers' money. Keeping Mark in jail for life will cost the public at least twenty thousand dollars a year. In ten years, that money could have paid for five college educations, thousands of school lunches, or countless vaccinations.

After her brother was sentenced to a five-year prison term for growing marijuana plants, Julie Stewart founded the organization Families against Mandatory Minimums (FAMM). Besides helping prisoners and their families appeal harsh drug sentences, FAMM has lobbied for less Draconian drug sentencing. "Members of Congress hold the key to changing the law," explains Stewart. "They could do it in a day, if they were so motivated." Adds Stewart, "It's not the procedure of appeal that stops them. . . . It's the fear of being labeled soft on crime."[7]

And so it goes. A change in sentencing rules is unlikely to occur until politicians and the constituents who elect them have a change of heart.

CHAPTER 4

Are the Drug Laws Enforceable?

Our jails are overcrowded, our judicial system overburdened, and our prison population is 1.6 million—more than any other industrial nation in the world. Catching criminals carries a huge price tag. Between the federal agencies, prosecutors, courts, and jails, Americans now spend 30 billion dollars trying to enforce the drug laws.[1] Despite these efforts, millions of Americans use drugs anyway.

One reason the drug laws are difficult to enforce is the number of citizens who violate them. Even if drug law enforcement focused solely on hard-core drug users and dealers, that would still amount to several million people—more than the population of most American cities.

Another reason drug laws are difficult to enforce is that they involve what legal scholars refer to as "victimless crimes." (Victimless does not imply that drug use has no victims—for it does—only that there are no victims in the legal sense.) Both the buyer and seller in a drug deal are guilty and therefore unlikely to report the crime. This, in turn, places the burden on the police, who must rely on witnesses to report drug crimes or pressure criminals to turn each other in or do their own undercover work.

Many witnesses refuse to assist authorities in finding and prosecuting dealers out of fear of the dealers' revenge. For example, one housing project resident knew of two apartments where crack was being sold. She withheld the information from the police because when she had given them tips previously, drug dealers had beaten up her daughter. After a grocer in a Florida neighborhood worked with police to catch drug dealers, he was shot to death.

It can take months, even years, to arrest a drug dealer or break up a drug ring. Long hours of vigilance are required—watching drug dealers come and go, listening to their telephone conversations, rummaging through their trash—before enough evidence can be gathered to make an arrest. Today's narcotics detectives must often be foot soldiers in the trenches. For a typical raid of three apartments where crack was suspected of being dealt, forty armed agents were required to batter down the apartment doors and surprise the occupants before they had time to get rid of evidence or reach for their weapons.

Less complicated but equally dangerous are undercover operations, in which agents pose as drug buyers (buy-and-bust) or drug dealers (sell-and-bust). Once a transaction is completed, the deal is used as evidence, and the agent arrests the person who sold or bought the drug.

To succeed at undercover work, agents must win the trust of the people they hope to arrest. Jerry O. was an undercover agent who would buy drugs from dealers then arrest them. One buy-and-bust cost him his spleen, half his liver, and part of his pancreas, when two dealers whose trust he had failed to earn robbed and shot him.

Keeping Drugs from the Market

A large supply of marijuana, LSD, and other drugs are grown or manufactured within the United States, but a much greater supply enters the country from foreign sources, carried across our national borders by drug runners. Preventing drugs from entering the U.S. is called inter-

Police on a drug raid

diction. However, it is virtually impossible to seal the country's borders completely, and huge quantities of drugs are smuggled in.

Drug runners show cunning in their efforts. In 1993, drug agents discovered a 1,400-foot (427 m) tunnel running from Tijuana, Mexico, to the outskirts of San Diego, California, where smugglers loaded cocaine onto trucks bound for Los Angeles and other locations.[2] Built under an inconspicuous warehouse, the well-lighted, reinforced concrete tunnel could accommodate a small car.

In another bust, customs officials found nearly five pounds (2.2 kg) of cocaine surgically implanted in the abdomen of a sheepdog shipped from Colombia to New York.[3] Drugs have also been concealed in trailers containing smelly fish, sewn into stuffed toy animals, and hidden in fuel tanks and mufflers.

With drug dealers' resourcefulness and the enormous length of the country's borders, interdiction is an unrealized goal. The United States shares over five thousand miles of border with Canada and nearly two thousand miles with Mexico. Much of these borders are wilderness or desert. Another nine thousand miles of border lie on either coast, with more than three hundred ports of entry, besides miles of private beaches. The U.S. Customs Service has the task of patrolling those borders, with some assistance from the FBI, the DEA, and the Coast Guard. Yet there are never enough personnel to patrol the borders adequately. After all, nearly 500 million people enter or reenter the U.S. each year.

Customs officials have only enough resources to search 5 to 10 percent of cars entering the country.[4] Searching more would cause tremendous delays and backups—and would infringe on the rights of the law-abiding people trying to cross the border.

Destroy the Supply before It Gets to the Market

One way to prevent the flow of drugs into the U.S. is to destroy illegal crops before they can be harvested and processed. This tactic, known as eradication, is performed by digging up the plants or, more often, by aerially spraying them with a chemical herbicide.

Eradication has a number of drawbacks. First, it is impossible to destroy every illegal poppy or marijuana plant on earth. Next, chemical eradication can cause harm to the environment. Finally, the chemicals used can harm people living nearby. After a decade of aerial eradication in Hawaii, some residents began complaining that the herbicide being used—glyphosate—was making them sick and killing wildlife. Apparently, the wind had blown the glyphosate into the roof catchments used by rural Hawaiians to collect rainwater for drinking. "You can actually taste it," said one resident.[5]

Eradication has backfired in other ways. In the U.S., it has spawned new techniques for growing marijuana. Some suppliers started growing their plants indoors. Some created hybrids that resemble corn, tomatoes, and other legal plants in order to escape detection.

Military Involvement

In 1879, Congress passed the *Posse Comitatus* Act to protect Americans from abuse by the military. The act stated that federal troops had no right to enter private land or dwellings or to detain or search civilians. A century later, Congress repealed the act.

In 1992 alone, the National Guard entered 1,230 privately owned buildings, intruded onto 2,500 private properties, and searched 120,000 cars for illegal drugs.[6]

Former Los Angeles prosecutor Vincent Bugliosi argues that the use of the military could give us an edge in the war against drugs. In fact, he argues, if Congress truly believes that drugs are a threat to national security, then it is "the *explicit constitutional duty* [Bugliosi's italics] of this nation's chief executive to pursue this course of action."[7] Bugliosi is not proposing a military invasion, such as when twenty thousand American troops invaded Panama to flush out General Manuel Noriega, the Panamanian leader charged with drug dealing. Rather, Bugliosi suggests that the U.S. military conduct "very limited search-and-find missions" to ferret out drug kingpins in Latin America and other foreign drug-producing areas.

No matter how limited the invasion, any military mission, especially one against ruthless drug lords, carries risks of injury and death. Moreover, if civilian law enforcement agents, with the use of semiautomatic weapons, have failed to stop organized drug dealing in the United States, can military troops accomplish that goal relying on more destructive weapons, perhaps bombs? Furthermore, a military invasion, however small, may escalate into a larger, more dangerous conflict.

Admittedly, drug laws are difficult, maybe impossible, to enforce. But are we ready to become a nation in which military personnel are used to enforce our civil laws? And are we willing to risk the chance that a small-scale invasion could lead to a large-scale conflict?

The Burden on Our Courts and Prisons

Arrests for drug crimes have increased enormously in the last two decades of drug prohibition. In 1996, 1.6 million people were living behind bars; another 3.5 million were on probation or parole. In 1960, only 5 percent (of a much smaller prison population) of prisoners were confined for drug crimes. By 1996, 25 percent of prisoners were incarcerated on drug charges. And many others were serving terms for theft and other crimes committed to support their drug habit.[8]

New drug laws and tougher enforcement have resulted in more arrests and longer incarceration. In 1996, 1.6 million people were arrested for a drug law violation—a 50 percent increase in just five years.[9]

No matter how acute the shortage of jail cells and how truncated the sentencing process, the system manages to lock up a remarkable number of prisoners for a democracy. For every 100,000 people:

- Japan has 37 prisoners

- Germany has 80

- Singapore has 229

- the United States has 600[10]

Neither the courts nor the prisons can keep pace with so many arrests and incarcerations. Many prisons are operating well beyond their capacity. To remedy overcrowding, a few localities have instituted a "prison cap," meaning that when the prisons are filled, only those charged with violent crimes such as rape and assault go to jail.

Because of overcrowding, many people who *should* be serving time for violent crimes are released before their sentences are complete. In some Texas cities, prisoners serve only one month for every twelve months of their sentence before being released on parole. In areas with acute overcrowding, prisoners may never be locked up for their sentence but are put on probation instead.

Bitter Fruits of the Drug Laws

Many critics of the drug laws believe that jailing an addict (unless he or she has committed another crime of *malum in se*) for possession of a drug is cruel and unusual punishment, that it harkens back to the days when insane or mentally retarded citizens were locked away.

Drug laws have created a new prison population of nonviolent offenders. Along the way they have also deprived a huge number of babies and young children of their parents. "We have taken a person off the street who is a junkie and we've made him a felon," laments a Legal Aid Society lawyer. "What have we accomplished? We've jammed our system and we haven't solved the drug problem."

Nor can bars keep prisoners from using drugs. Those who used them before their arrest continue using them while incarcerated, finding them almost as easy to get in prison as on the street.

In a national poll of police

U. S. Prison Population
- 5.1 million people in criminal justice system in 1995.
- 1.6 million in federal and state prisons and local jails.
- 3.5 million on probation and parole.
- One-third of drug law violators were nonviolent offenders with little or no criminal history; two-thirds of these received mandatory minimum sentences.
- Drug offenders make up 60 percent of the federal prison population and 25 percent of state and local prison populations.

Source: Bureau of Justice Statistics

*Only 6 percent of prison inmates are female, but many
have children.*

chiefs, 59 percent believed court-supervised treatment programs are
more effective than prison or jail time.[11] As many as four out of five
arrestees in some cities test positive for drugs at the time of their arrest.[12]
Yet fewer than 2 percent of drug offenders receive any kind of drug
treatment or enter prevention programs as part of their sentence. Even

if treatment is available, it is not always offered. When New York State opened a residential treatment center for felons, hundreds of its beds remained empty because prosecutors refused to let prisoners participate. They thought the three-month program was too short to rehabilitate a second-time offender.[13]

There is an especially acute shortage of treatment options for women with children, and one in three female prisoners is in prison for drug charges.[14] In fact, the trend is to arrest, convict, and jail pregnant women addicted to drugs in order to get them off drugs before they give birth. But does jailing these women instead of offering them treatment truly benefit society? As one critic suggested, "Their punishment should fit the crime, not destroy the family unit."[15]

Our courts are as overburdened as the jails and prisons. There simply aren't nearly enough prosecutors, judges, courtrooms, laboratories, or grand juries to handle the huge volume of drug arrests.

Drug cases place an especially heavy burden on the judicial system because they are massive and complex. A typical case takes several months in court. A backlog of cases causes a delay in arraignments (where an arrested person is charged with a crime). Since many defendants must remain in jail until their arraignment, taxpayers foot the bill for the delay. In addition, these delays cause serious infringements of a person's right to a speedy arraignment and trial.

Decriminalizing or legalizing drugs could ease the burden now placed on the justice system but will not eliminate it. Drug misuse contributes to family violence. In New York City, for example, crack addiction caused a tripling of the number of cases in which parents abused or neglected their children. The majority of all juvenile cases, in fact, result from abuse or neglect by parents abusing drugs, both legal and illegal. These cases will continue to burden the judicial system, and the number may increase if drugs such as cocaine are legalized.

Judging by recent records, law enforcement agencies are now more effective at making drug arrests, destroying illegal crops, and seizing illegal drugs. Despite the improved record, though, drug use remains widespread. The courts and prisons remain buried under drug cases, and domestic violence and neglect stemming from drug abuse remain all too common.

Concerned about these problems, 85 percent of the police chiefs responding to a national poll called for a change in the way we enforce the drug laws. Nonetheless, 90 percent believed that legalization or decriminalization is the wrong direction to take.

One way to ease the burden on the criminal justice system would be to change the mandatory sentencing rules and to offer treatment-on-demand to first-time drug offenders. This would improve drug users' chances of staying out of the system in the future.

No doubt, it is possible to improve the record on enforcement. Winning the war on drugs probably requires more than the billions already spent, including more law enforcement agents than we already have. That path, however, could double, or even triple, the already swollen prison population, as well as put millions more on probation and parole. Do we want to live in a society that makes so many of its citizens wards of the state?

If marijuana alone were decriminalized or legalized, we could reduce the number of arrests by five hundred thousand a year. This would allow law enforcement agents to focus more on violent crime. On the other hand, changing the drug laws or enforcing them better are not our only alternatives. Why not work to do a better job at preventing drug abuse? Why not offer effective treatment to every person who needs or wants it, especially to those we incarcerate for drug violations?

CHAPTER 5

Do Drug Laws Step on Civil Liberties?

Two young men left their homes in Pennsylvania for a vacation in Jamaica.[1] On their return to Newark Airport, they were surrounded by U.S. customs agents, put into separate rooms, and strip-searched. When the search (conducted without a warrant) yielded no evidence of guilt, they were handcuffed and transported to a nearby hospital, where they were shackled to beds by their ankles.

Next, the weary travelers were X-rayed to determine if they had swallowed any drugs. A suspicious-looking object appeared in one man's X rays, and he was ordered to take a laxative and remain chained to the bed until he produced a bowel movement. When the customs agents finally were convinced that he was innocent, he was released. Later, both men received bills from the hospital for use of its facilities.

Why were the two men singled out? Airline passengers who appear nervous or in a hurry, or travel without luggage, especially on flights to Miami, Detroit, and Houston, are routinely searched. Having the *appearance* of a drug courier has never been clearly defined, but people of color, as were the travelers to Jamaica, are singled out more often than other people. At the Memphis airport, for instance, three out of four black travelers are stopped, although only 4 percent of the flying public is black.[2]

Motorists are routinely stopped and searched, especially those driving cars with license plates from states with thriving illegal drug markets, such as Florida or Texas; those traveling near international borders; or young people driving late-model cars through high drug-traffic areas.[3]

Hard drugs and related crime seriously disrupt many lives and destroy many neighborhoods. But in the zeal to fight drug crime, law enforcement policies sacrifice some of our basic civil rights, from the right of due process and protection from searches without warrants, to the right to use drugs in spiritual or religious practices. "Throughout [American] history, the government has said we're in an unprecedented crisis and that we must live without civil liberties until the crisis is over," observes Yale Kamisar, a law professor at the University of Michigan. "It's a hoax," he retorts.[4]

Is Our Right to Privacy Being Eroded?

The right of the people to be secure in their persons, houses, papers, and effects, against unreasonable searches and seizures, shall not be violated, and no warrants shall issue, but upon probable cause, supported by oath or affirmation, and particularly describing the place to be searched, and the persons or things to be seized.

—the Fourth Amendment

The Fourth Amendment to the Constitution is supposed to protect citizens from unlawful search and seizure. As the drug war intensifies, though, the boundaries between lawful and unlawful are being eroded. In fact, recent Supreme Court decisions have raised serious concern about those rights.

According to the Fourth Amendment, law officers are required to justify their search and obtain a search warrant before looking for drugs. They are also required to knock and announce their presence before entering a home to execute a search warrant, a custom deeply imbedded in English legal doctrine dating back to the Middle Ages. Nonetheless, in 1995 and 1997 rulings, the Supreme Court stated that in certain circumstances police may conduct searches without warrants.[5]

Without a person's consent, police may inspect personal bank records, record telephone numbers dialed from a person's home, and tape telephone and personal conversations. They may inspect a person's trash. They may set up roadblocks and stop drivers to search their cars.

In the early 1970s, a U.S. Drug Enforcement Agency officer developed a profile of drug runners for use in airports, train stations, and on highways by federal, state, and local law enforcement agents. Anyone thought to fit the profile can be "Terry stopped," based on *Terry v. Ohio*, a 1968 case in which the U.S. Supreme Court held that police could stop and frisk a person merely if the person's conduct gave rise to "an apprehension of danger."[6]

In 1989, the Supreme Court continued to rule that the procedure was legal. However, Justice Thurgood Marshall dissented: "Reliance on a profile of drug courier characteristics runs a far greater risk than does ordinary, case-by-case police work of subjecting innocent individuals to unwarranted police harassment and detention."[7]

That same year in another case, the Court ruled that a person's behavior and not just appearance has to rouse suspicion. Nonetheless, many officials go on appearance alone. Or they have such a broad definition of suspicious behavior that just about anyone is subject to search—particularly if they are members of a minority.

At airport baggage areas, dogs are used to sniff out drugs.

In the Name of Law and Order

In 1981, the General Accounting Office issued a report, "Asset Forfeiture: A Seldom Used Tool in Combatting Drug Trafficking," reminding law enforcement agents that certain state and federal civil forfeiture laws give the government the right to seize property—including cash, homes, and vehicles—used for or purchased from illegal activity. The owners need not be convicted or even charged with a crime. Mere suspicion is sufficient, and the burden is on the owners to prove themselves innocent.

Between 1986 and 1991, the U.S. Justice Department took in more than $1.5 billion worth of forfeitures. By 1993, they had accumulated nearly $2 billion worth of real property, including office buildings, luxury waterfront homes, farms, and crack houses in the slums, which had been taken on the suspicion that they were bought with money from illegal activities.[8]

The justice system is based on the premise that a person is innocent until proven guilty. Yet in 80 percent of the DEA's successful forfeitures, the owners of the property were never charged with a crime. It can take ten to fifteen thousand dollars in legal fees to recover a car. Many people, including some who are innocent but unable to afford such legal fees, decide not to contest the seizure, which allows the government to keep their property.

During one search, police found fifteen thousand dollars in drug money stashed in a safe and a small amount of cocaine under a couch cushion. The money belonged to the grandson of the woman who lived in the house. She knew nothing about the money or her grandson's drug dealings and was innocent of any crime. Because drug money was found on her premises, under forfeiture provisions of federal law, the house was placed "under arrest." The woman, her daughter, her grandchildren, and her great-grandchild were all ordered to leave.[9]

Similarly, when a single marijuana cigarette was found in the crew's quarters of the *Atlantis*, an oceanographic research vessel, the entire ship was seized. In another incident, a teenager loaned the family car to a friend. When police found a single roach, the car was taken.

Testing for Drug Use

Many employers—the military, businesses with government contracts, transportation and utility companies, even some small establishments like video stores—routinely screen employees for drugs. There isn't a life insurance company that does not require policy applicants to take a test for drug use. Today, parents can test their unsuspecting children by sending a snippet of hair to a lab for analysis. During his 1996 reelection campaign, President Clinton proposed that teenagers pass a drug test before receiving a driver's license.

Drug testing raises several questions: Are drug tests an unwarranted search? Do they invade a person's privacy? Are they reliable?

On March 21, 1989, the Supreme Court first ruled on drug testing of employees. In *Skinner v. Railway Labor Executives*, the Court upheld drug testing as a way to ensure public safety. In the majority opinion, Justice Anthony Kennedy wrote that the tests were indeed "searches." They were reasonable searches, however, because operating rail equipment while drug impaired creates risks for both the passengers and the workers. In a dissenting opinion, Justice Thurgood Marshall accused the Court's majority of allowing itself to be "swept away by society's obsession with stopping the scourge of illegal drugs. . . . History teaches that grave threats to liberty often come in times of urgency, when constitutional rights seem too extravagant to endure." He continued, "There is no drug exception to the Constitution."

In 1995, the parents of a seventh-grade student who refused to be subjected to random drug testing of football players challenged the practice. When the case was appealed to the Ninth District Court in San Francisco, the judge ruled against testing. "Children are compelled to attend school, but nothing suggests that they lose their right to privacy in their excretory functions," wrote Judge Ferdinand R. Fernandez.[10]

Other states, including Colorado, have also declared such testing unconstitutional. When the California case reached the Supreme Court in 1995, however, the majority upheld the legality of random drug testing of school athletes.

Defenders of drug testing claim that given the design of public urinals and locker-room showers and the way we are routinely subjected to urine and bowel tests during physical exams, our privacy is frequently invaded. Testing for drugs, the Court reasoned in its majority opinion, does not go beyond these routine and acceptable invasions.

Another concern in drug testing is accuracy. Tests can indicate that a drug is present in the body, but its effects on a person's job performance may be long gone. For example, on Friday night, a person can smoke marijuana. On Monday morning, the effect of the drug has worn off, but since marijuana can be detected for approximately thirty days after use, the person will test positive. So if the issue is a person's ability to perform, the drug test raises a false alarm.

Drug use can also elude the test. Cocaine cannot be detected two days after use. An employee heavily abusing it over the weekend can show up for work, take a urine test, and pass with the cocaine undetected. Persons using PCP (angel dust) may remain paranoid and delusional days after the drug is detectable.[11]

People who don't take illegal substances sometimes test positive. Certain drugs taken for muscle aches or arthritis are legal and may be purchased over the counter or with a prescription. However, they may show up as marijuana in a urine test, giving a false positive.[12]

Finally, people who use drugs can substitute urine samples that are not their own or add a substance to make their test negative when it would otherwise register positive. For this reason, many urine tests are now conducted in view of a supervisor. "Hey," said one irate employee, "how would you like to pee in front of your boss?"

Drug testing may step on civil rights, but it does stop many people from using drugs, especially if their jobs are on the line. When the U.S. military discovered widespread drug use among returning Vietnam veterans, it began testing for drugs. Then, in 1981, the tests were performed on everyone, from recruits to officers. In 1980, 27 percent of military personnel had been found to have used drugs. Once testing began, the figure dropped to 19 percent, and by 1985 it was a third of the original rate—9 percent.[13] Perhaps the threat that a surprise urine test may lead to the loss of a job deters people from using drugs—or from applying for jobs that require drug testing.

Is the success of drug testing, whether limited or substantial, worth the erosion of civil rights? Yes, voted the Supreme Court, though not unanimously. Justice Antonin Scalia believes that unreasonable searches can never be justified, regardless of the cause. Apparently though, Justice Scalia does not extend that right to student athletes; in 1995 he wrote the majority opinion defending a school's right to random testing of its student athletes.

Live and Let Live

In April 1995, a revival of a play by French writer and filmmaker Jean Cocteau opened in New York. Vincent Canby, a *New York Times* theater critic, wrote, "It's easy to believe that he [Cocteau] wrote *Les Parents Terribles* during an eight-day opium binge. This is not a play that was worried into existence, developed over time, composed of bits and pieces from notebooks, or whipped into shape out of town. It has the eerie seamlessness, the tight construction, and the density of a work composed in one spontaneous rush of imagination."[14]

Cocteau and some other artists, writers, musicians, and scientists have used drugs, believing they would enhance their creativity or increase their productivity. The list of reported drug users includes Sigmund Freud, Billie Holiday, Louis Armstrong, and the Beatles. Whether the drugs (of various types) had positive or negative effects is not certain.

It can be argued that the works—as well as the relationships, health, and private lives—of many drug users suffer as a result of drug use and misuse. Further, creative ability and genius do not require experience with "artificial paradise" in order to produce works of art or make important discoveries. Yet does the government have the right to deny anyone—brilliant, creative, or otherwise—the right to use drugs? Indeed, what right does government have to decide what we can and cannot do?

Legal drugs, such as wine, have been used in religious ceremonies for thousands of years. It is hard to imagine a Catholic Communion service or a Jewish Passover Seder without wine. But, according to our current drug laws, those who consider drugs such as peyote, psychedelic mushrooms, or marijuana to have sacramental use in their religion are not free to use them.

James Lee and his wife, Anyatika, are Nazarites, whose beliefs are similar to those of the Rastafarians, a religious sect from Jamaica. Like Rastafarians, the Nazarites espouse peace and love and refrain from eating meat or dairy products. In addition, they do not take aspirin or prescription drugs or drink alcoholic beverages. Also like Rastafarians, Nazarites consider marijuana an essential part of their religious practice. "I don't get high," explains Lee. "I get centered in God. It's a very big difference."[15]

Although the Religious Freedom Restoration Act of 1993 guarantees the freedom to practice religion as protected by the Constitution, religious sects that use illicit drugs are excluded from such protection.

Besides religious and mind-expanding reasons, some people use drugs casually, to relax, socialize, or escape the pain in their lives. Remember that nearly 80 million Americans have used an illegal drug at least once. In 1995 alone, almost 12 million admitted to using drugs.[16] Does our government have the right to legislate this kind of moral behavior for its citizens?

In 1859, in his essay *On Liberty*, John Stuart Mill advised free societies and their governments to protect the individual's rights. Wrote Mill: "The only purpose for which power can be rightfully exercised over any member of a civilized community, against his will, is to prevent harm to others. His own good, either physical or moral, is not sufficient warrant."

When the question was put before the Alaskan state supreme court in 1976, every one of the justices agreed that the possession of marijuana, by adults at home for personal use, is protected by their constitutional right to privacy. Wrote Justice Jay Rabinowitz in *Ravin v. State of Alaska,* "Big Brother cannot in the name of public health dictate to anyone what he can eat or drink or smoke in the privacy of his own home."

Reflecting on Mill's advice, Stephen Wisotsky, a legal scholar, claims that a "democratic society must respect the decisions made by its adult citizens, even those perceived as foolish or risky."[17] In a free society,

Some people believe they have a right to use drugs without government interference.

people take many risks. They smoke cigarettes, rock climb, and bungee jump without breaking the law. Of course, critics point out that hard drugs are harmful—both to users and those affected by their behavior.

"Paternalism" is a term applied to laws that are passed to protect citizens from harm. One example of paternalism is the law that requires cyclists to wear helmets. If the occasional use of drugs such as marijuana or cocaine gives users pleasure, what right does government have to say they are illegal?

John Kaplan, author of a book about heroin addiction, agreed that Mill's belief that government should stay out of private affairs is appealing. "But it does not work in the real world," observed Kaplan, "where a cyclist without a helmet can crash and end up the public's ward in some nursing home."[18] If society is expected to provide minimal food, shelter, medical help, and other necessary services for its citizens, including addicts who are too down-and-out to provide for themselves, shouldn't society have the right to pass laws to prevent addiction in the first place? As with other difficult issues, each side of the argument causes another side to sacrifice. As one critic of the law reasons, "If getting high means that a person with AIDS can sit down to eat dinner with friends and loved ones or get a full night's sleep, what's wrong with getting high?"[19]

The Call for Common Sense

The other side of the issue of paternalism is this argument: If government *does* have a responsibility to protect its citizens, why won't the federal government extend that protection to IV drug users? The Department of Health and Human Services estimates that twenty thousand Americans contract HIV each year by sharing needles.[20] Supplying addicts with sterile syringes and needles can deter the spread of HIV, hepatitis, and other communicable diseases and may spare thousands of babies from being born HIV-positive. On what grounds does the federal government reject such a pragmatic (and perhaps, humane) policy?

In 1992, Connecticut made it legal for pharmacies to sell syringes to addicts without prescriptions. The rate of HIV infection among drug users fell by 40 percent.[21] In New Jersey, where such sales are not permitted, the spread of HIV is three and a half times greater than in states that allow them.[22] In Dallas and New Orleans, IV drug users can buy needles over the counter. By 1992, 2 percent of intravenous drug users in these cities were infected with HIV. In New York City and Newark, New Jersey, where drug users could not purchase clean needles over the counter, the 1992 rate of HIV infection was 50 to 60 percent.[23] Granted, many IV drug users would fail to take advantage of clean-needle programs. After all, hard drugs attract people who take risks.

Opponents fear that needle exchange programs and legal syringes encourage drug addicts to stay on drugs. They also claim that this policy seems to sanction IV drug use and sends the wrong message.

In 1995, Congress commissioned a fifteen-member panel of experts to research the issue. As with earlier studies, they concluded that needle programs can stem the spread of HIV and other communicable diseases and, furthermore, that drug use among participants does not increase. The panel recommended that Congress fund needle exchanges.[24] Yet the government failed to follow the advice. With limited access to clean needles, drug users continue to spread HIV—to themselves, their sexual partners, and their offspring.

A Just Society

Deeply intertwined with the drug issue is an issue of ethics: What is right and what is wrong, what are our rights, and what constitutes a just society? In a perfect society, no one would step on the rights of anyone else or abuse themselves. The challenge facing our society, and each rational member of it, is to create a society in which democracy prevails.

A dark period of our recent history was the McCarthy era, during the Cold War with the Soviet Union, when fear of Communism caused many Americans to "name names." In an effort to sweep America clean of anyone suspected of sympathizing with the communist movement, citizens, especially those in the Defense Department, the theater, movies, and literature, were questioned about themselves and the loyalty of their acquaintances by a congressional committee led by Senator Joseph McCarthy. At times, people provided names out of a misguided sense of patriotism. Sometimes they named people they barely knew in order to save themselves from persecution, jail, or worse.

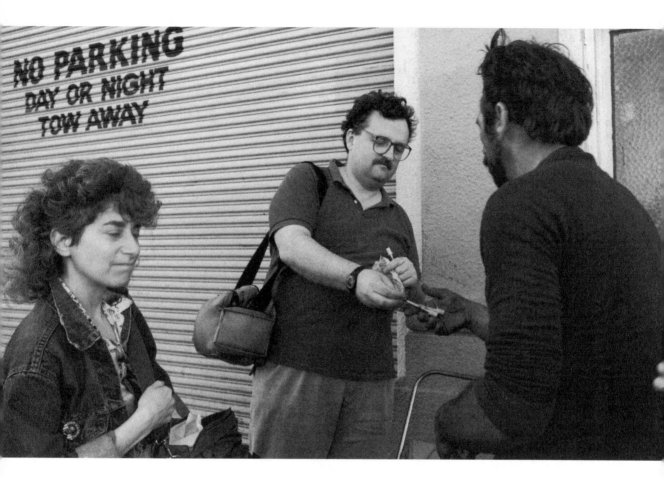

In 1996, the United States had a hundred needle exchange programs. Australia, with one-tenth the population, had two thousand.

To an extent, a similar wave of fear has swept the nation over drugs, crime, and violence. People are once again being encouraged to name names. Under the well-meaning drug education program DARE, for example, young people may be encouraged to report on drug use in their families. After thirteen-year-old Crystal G. told a DARE officer that her parents smoked pot, the officer used the information to justify a search of her home. When marijuana plants were discovered, her parents were arrested. "This is the stuff of Orwellian fiction," says Gary Peterson, head of Parents against DARE, a Fort Collins, Colorado, group. "This is Big Brother putting spies in our homes."[25]

When charged with a drug crime and faced with long, mandatory sentencing, a suspect may have a sentence reduced by naming other persons who are involved in illegal drug activity. To critics, this arrangement echoes McCarthyism and repressive governments, in which citizens are pressured (or rewarded) for squealing on their acquaintances. In short, winning the drug war by asking people to name names makes those who remember the lessons of history cringe. For them, the ends cannot justify the means, no matter how worthy the goal appears to be.

On a final note, consider this: Cigarettes kill far more citizens than drugs or the guns that drug dealers fire. Prescription drugs, such as antidepressants, are responsible for a third of the drug overdoses that turn up in hospital emergency rooms each year, which is three times the rate of heroin overdoses.[26] The current drug policy encourages society to view people who use drugs, and especially those who are dependent on drugs, as criminals. Why not change our perspective and offer drug abusers—including those who have committed a crime—treatment, tolerance, and compassion?

CHAPTER 6

A Medical Alternative

In 1971, Robert C. Randall was diagnosed with glaucoma. His doctor predicted that within three to five years he would be blind as a result of the pressure on his optic nerves. He prescribed drugs to reduce the pressure, but Randall found little relief. The glaucoma continued to create pressure in his eyes, distorting his vision and causing him to see tricolored halos.

One night Randall smoked some marijuana to relax and noticed that the halos disappeared and his vision improved. During the next months, he smoked marijuana again and again. He came to believe that in order to save his eyesight, he would need a steady source of marijuana—and an affordable one. Randall started growing six marijuana plants. Then, while he was away on a vacation, a neighbor reported the plants to the police. When Randall returned, he was greeted by the vice squad and charged with a crime.

A two-year legal battle followed. While researching his defense,

Randall talked to employees at the federal government's National Institute on Drug Abuse (NIDA), the Federal Drug Agency (FDA), and the Drug Enforcement Agency (DEA). A few employees believed that marijuana could help glaucoma patients and indicated that the agencies had withheld this information. Randall set out to persuade the federal government to supply him with marijuana. He underwent medical tests at UCLA's medical center where his doctor concluded that with conventional drug therapy, Randall would go blind or would need risky eye surgery. The doctor also concluded that marijuana could prolong Randall's eyesight.

Based on this medical recommendation and further tests, Randall petitioned the federal government for access to its legal supply of marijuana grown at the University of Mississippi. At first the DEA refused the request, saying, "Randall is a criminal."[1] However, both NIDA and the FDA agreed that if a physician would submit a formal application to the Investigational New Drug (IND) program at the FDA, they would supply Randall with marijuana.

After surmounting additional obstacles, in 1976 Randall secured a government supply of marijuana cigarettes. Four years later, he became the cofounder and president of the Alliance for Cannabis Therapeutics (ACT), an organization that seeks to make marijuana legally available for legitimate medical uses. In 1997, the government was still supplying him with ten marijuana cigarettes a day, rolled by the federal government's official supplier—the University of Mississippi. Randall believes that marijuana has enabled him to retain his sight and that without it, he would have gone blind.

Many other people use marijuana for debilitating medical conditions. C. Fred McBee, a member of the disabled community, explains, "To call marijuana's therapeutic use within the paralyzed community widespread would be an understatement. Marijuana is not simply the drug of choice among many paralyzed Americans. It is the only drug that provides us with effective, nondebilitating relief from spasms and pain, and permits us to function as competent individuals who work regular jobs and actively participate in society."[2]

Medical Use of Marijuana

In California, a young mother with multiple sclerosis (MS) was bedridden, too nauseated to hold down food, and suffered from severe muscle spasms and twitching. Prescription drugs provided little relief. After she began smoking marijuana, she regained her appetite, stopped having spasms, and after three months, was able to walk again and care for her young children.[3]

Ara C. of Wichita, Kansas, was diagnosed with a form of chronic glaucoma. Her doctor suggested surgery to reduce the pressure on her optic nerve. After hearing about the medicinal effect of marijuana, Ara tried it and it seemed to work. Ara's doctor tested her eye pressure before and after smoking. After smoking, it fell to the "safe" range. This persuaded her doctor to seek federal approval to prescribe marijuana for Ara. Yet the FDA repeatedly ignored the doctor's requests. Without a supply of marijuana, Ara was compelled to have surgery. Surgery failed, and Ara lost her remaining reading vision.

Marijuana is a natural herb that has been used in medicine for thousands of years. According to Lester Grinspoon, a physician and the author of *Marijuana: The Forbidden Medicine*, it has numerous medical uses, some of which are unduplicated by any other substance.

Epilepsy (brain seizures). A million people in the United States have epilepsy. For nearly one out of five of these people, no drug stops their seizures entirely. Smoking marijuana has helped some of them reduce the amount of antiseizure drugs they need, while others have found that marijuana controls their seizures.

Glaucoma. Between two and eight million Americans have glaucoma, an eye disease in which pressure in the eye causes blindness. A number of glaucoma patients have claimed that marijuana lessens the pressure. For some of the 10 to 20 percent of glaucoma patients for

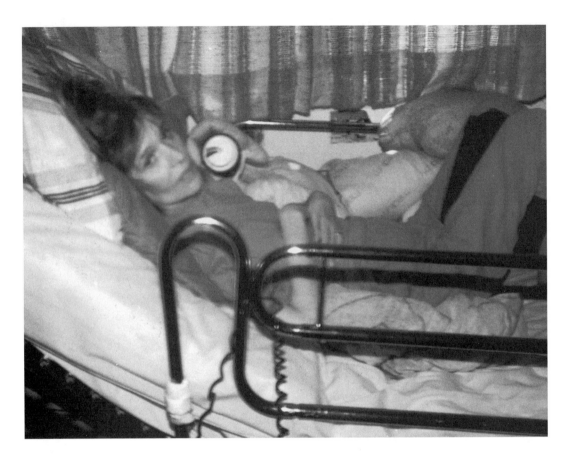

This person, who suffers from MS, has repeatedly tried and failed to get a legal supply of marijuana from the government.

whom current medical treatments fail, marijuana seems their only hope to avoid blindness or surgery that may result in blindness.

Muscle spasms and pain. Marijuana can reduce the muscle jerking and spasms that people with cerebral palsy, multiple sclerosis, and paralysis experience. In addition, it may help restore some lost muscle control, especially of the bladder.

Marijuana can diminish the severe pain of rheumatoid arthritis and migraines and the itching of pruritis, a skin inflammation that can lead to gangrene (decay of body tissue).

AIDS and cancer. Many AIDS patients suffer from rapid loss of weight. Because marijuana can improve a person's appetite and decrease nausea and vomiting, it can help people with AIDS maintain their appetites as well as deal with the side effects of AZT (a drug used to treat HIV and AIDS). Because it is an effective antinausea drug, marijuana is also used by cancer patients undergoing chemotherapy or radiation treatment.

Thousands of people smoke marijuana to treat these serious medical conditions. Marijuana is a Schedule I drug, which means that doctors cannot prescribe it. The sole legal source of medical marijuana is through the Investigational Drug Program (IDP), and by 1996 only eight patients were allowed to receive marijuana through the program. All the others who use marijuana medically resort to illegal sources and thus risk arrest. If they choose to buy illegal marijuana, they can pay five thousand dollars or more for a year's supply. Those unwilling to break the law, unable to find a source, or unable to pay for the marijuana, will miss the benefits it may offer them.

At nineteen, Valerie C. received a traumatic brain injury in a car accident. She suffered numerous grand mal epileptic seizures. To control the seizures, powerful depressants that put her into a constant stupor were prescribed. "It was much like living under water," Valerie explains. "The drugs did not relieve the pain. They either knocked me out or put a kind of veil over me." After reading in a medical journal that marijuana had interrupted seizures in laboratory rats, Valerie tried smoking it. She discovered that her seizures stopped, and fifteen years later, Valerie has not experienced another seizure.

Valerie began working with terminally ill patients, supplying them with marijuana to help ease their pain. After years of distributing marijuana, however, she and her husband were arrested. People like Valerie caught growing or distributing marijuana—regardless of the reason—may face penalties.

Hard Questions

A federal policy that prohibits physicians from alleviating suffering by prescribing marijuana for seriously ill patients is misguided, heavy-handed, and inhumane. . . . It is also hypocritical to forbid physicians to prescribe marijuana while permitting them to use morphine. . . . The government should change marijuana's status from that of a Schedule 1 drug (considered to be potentially addictive and with no current medical use) to that of a Schedule 2 drug (potentially addictive but with some accepted medical use) and regulate it accordingly.

—New England Journal of Medicine[4]

The list of organizations that endorse the medical use of marijuana is long—and growing. It includes

- American Academy of Family Physicians

- American Bar Association

- American Medical Students Association

- California Medical Association

- California Nurses Association

- Lymphoma Foundation of America

- National Association of Attorneys General

- Virginia Nurses Association

- Physicians Association for AIDS Care

If marijuana is effective, why isn't it available for medical use? Many opponents fear that if marijuana is made available for cancer, AIDS, and

MS patients, it will soon be available for everyone. Some also believe that teenagers, in particular, will see less harm in the casual use of marijuana if it is deemed valuable for medical use. The argument has logic but little empathy for the many sick, injured, or hurting people who could benefit from marijuana.

Opinion is divided on the medical use of marijuana. Despite personal testimonies and studies that show marijuana's effectiveness, the Drug Enforcement Agency and many physicians want more proof. Furthermore, for patients with blood pressure problems or those who have a mental illness such as schizophrenia, marijuana can be detrimental. Also, some experts believe that long-term marijuana use might depress the immune system, which can be harmful and dangerous for AIDS patients and those on chemotherapy, who are susceptible to pneumonia and other aggressive infections. Finally, smoking marijuana over a long period of time may damage the lungs and bronchial tubes.

Compared to many other drugs used medically, marijuana is relatively safe. It has few of the dangerous side effects of drugs used to tranquilize people, stop vomiting, relieve pain, and relax muscle spasms. Nor are there reports of people dying of an overdose of marijuana.

The toxicity (degree of being poisonous) of a drug can be measured and assigned a numerical rating, called an LD (lethal dosage). Many of the drugs used for cancer chemotherapy are extremely toxic and have a rating as low as LD 1.5. This means that taking just half again as much as the prescribed dosage—say, three pills instead of the prescribed two—could kill a person.

In contrast to these highly toxic drugs, marijuana has an LD of 20,000 to 40,000. This means that to cause death, a person would have to smoke 1,500 pounds (680 kg) of marijuana—720,000 joints—in fifteen minutes. As the father of a teenage cancer patient who used marijuana observed, "I have seen what chemotherapy drugs do to patients. . . . To pretend that marijuana is more dangerous than these lethal chemicals is sheer nonsense."[5]

Many medical experts concur. "I'm accused of recklessly telling people to try this drug [marijuana]," reasons Dr. Lester Grinspoon. "It would be reckless if there were serious consequences, but there aren't. People who try it have nothing to lose. If it works, they have a lot to gain."[6]

A Marijuana Substitute

A major reason for denying the medical use of marijuana is that since 1985 a synthetic form of THC—dronabinol—has been available under the trade name Marinol. Marinol is said to offer patients the same medical relief as marijuana. Unfortunately, for many patients, Marinol offers no relief or has such unpleasant side effects that they prefer not to take it.

Just as manufacturers of infant formula cannot duplicate breast milk and every one of its benefits, neither can drug companies duplicate marijuana. Marijuana contains nearly four hundred chemical compounds and sixty cannabanoids besides THC; Marinol is pure THC. It is possible that the additional compounds and cannabanoids in marijuana may contribute to the milder effect of marijuana.

Because marijuana is smoked, it rapidly enters the bloodstream from the lungs, and its effects can be felt within minutes. Marinol enters the body through the digestive system, a process that can take up to four hours. Since marijuana is smoked puff by puff, patients can regulate their dosage, which they cannot do with Marinol. And if someone is suffering from severe nausea and vomiting—often the reason for using marijuana—it may be impossible to swallow or retain a Marinol pill.

Marijuana may give patients a mild euphoria. With Marinol, some patients suffer frightening hallucinations, dizziness, disorientation, and anxiety, symptoms which can last as long as ten hours. Thus, while patients who have smoked marijuana can join their friends and families in socializing and eating soon after smoking, Marinol patients experience no such benefits.

Dr. Alfred Chang, who conducted a study comparing the effects of marijuana and Marinol in animals, wrote that "the marijuana cigarette may be the best means of administering the drug."[7] Later state programs comparing patients smoking marijuana with those on Marinol supported Dr. Chang's conclusion. Actually, a number of patients in the studies so detested the Marinol that they threw it away.

One final argument: Marinol is expensive. In 1997, a single Marinol capsule cost eight dollars. Legal marijuana is far less costly and easier to supply, especially if patients are allowed to grow their own.

The Legal Issue

Since its inception in 1978, the Investigational New Drug program has had the legal ability to allow the FDA to authorize marijuana use and to allow the DEA to supply it. However, as noted earlier, by 1996 only eight people were allowed to participate in the program.

During the 97th Congress (1981), four congressional members, including Newt Gingrich of Georgia, introduced bill H.R. 4498 to "provide for the therapeutic use of marijuana in situations involving life-threatening or sense-threatening illnesses, and to provide adequate supplies of marijuana for such use." When the bill emerged from committee for a vote, it had support from 71 representatives. When put to vote, though, H.R. 4498 met with defeat. Several other versions of a bill to legalize medical marijuana have been introduced. Even though one had 110 cosponsors, it, too, failed to pass.

In 1986, the DEA was given the task of analyzing the issue of medical marijuana. For two years Judge Francis J. Young listened to testimony about marijuana's medical use from doctors, medical personnel, parents of children who had used marijuana during medical treatment, and patients who had used marijuana to treat a range of serious medical conditions. Testimony from the hearings was compiled into the two-volume *Marijuana, Medicine, and the Law*.

At the conclusion of the hearings, Judge Young advised the DEA to reschedule marijuana and make it available by prescription. "The evidence in this record clearly shows that marijuana has been accepted as capable of relieving the distress of great numbers of very ill people, and doing so with safety under medical supervision," Judge Young stated. "It would be unreasonable, arbitrary, and capricious for the DEA to continue to stand between those sufferers and the benefit of this substance in light of the evidence in this record."[8]

Just as President Nixon had refused his commission's advice to decriminalize marijuana, DEA director John Lawn ignored the advice of his legal administrator. When Judge Young made the recommendation to the DEA, George Bush was president and was trying to make America drug free. Bush upheld Lawn's decision to ignore Judge Young's recommendation. In fact, Bush stopped the DEA from distributing the marijuana it had already promised to make available through the Investigational New Drug program. Those rejected included scores of patients dying of AIDS.

When President Clinton took office, he ignored an early campaign promise to make marijuana available to those who need it medically. Following Bush's lead, he upheld the ban.

Besides the federal government, state and local governments have put the issue on their agendas. The first state to address the issue was New Mexico. In 1978, a young man dying of testicular cancer lobbied New Mexico's state legislators who then voted overwhelmingly for a bill recognizing marijuana's medical value, which was signed into law by the governor. Due to federal delays in supplying the marijuana, the young man with cancer died before receiving a single "legal" marijuana cigarette. For a short while, though, about 250 patients received a legal supply of marijuana. And for nine out of ten of these patients, marijuana proved effective. Thirty-five other states have followed New Mexico's lead and enacted the bills with clear majorities.

A few city governments have also voted to allow the distribution of medical marijuana. These include Breckenridge, Colorado, and San Francisco and Santa Cruz, California.

The big test came in 1996, when the issue of medical marijuana was put to California and Arizona voters during the November general election. In both states, the issue won by a clear majority—collecting 56 percent of the vote in California and 65 percent in Arizona.

California's coalition of underground cannabis-buying clubs began seeking ways to get government support for the distribution of marijuana. Nonetheless, until the federal government, the Supreme Court, or a new amendment to the Constitution ends the ban on medical marijuana, it will, in essence, remain illegal. For no matter what occurs in the state or local legislatures, federal law is the "law of the land." Federal agents have the power to stop any and all distribution programs.

Down the Slippery Slope

The Office of National Drug Control Policy issued a press release after the passage of the California measure to legalize medical marijuana, voicing a concern shared by many other Americans: "The passage of [Proposition 215] creates a significant threat to the drug control system that protects our children."[9] As the statement shows, many people fear that if we reform the drug laws to allow for medical marijuana, we will "slide down a slippery slope" to permitting marijuana for recreational use. Further, legalization could also pave the way toward repeal of all drug laws and regulations.

Slippery-slope reasoning is tricky because of its apparent logic. After all, loosening up one area of drug reform *can* pave the way to reform in another. The fault in this reasoning is that the outcome is not inevitable. Legalizing marijuana so that young cancer patients can use it to relieve vomiting and nausea does not mean marijuana brownies will be served in the high school cafeteria.

On the other hand, the slippery-slope argument may contain some truth. If marijuana were legalized for medical purposes, it probably would be easier to obtain for recreational use. When the San Francisco buying club was shut down, the justification was that many people were falsifying medical conditions to be able to purchase marijuana at the club. As an illustration, critics cite Ritalin (a drug used for hyperactivity), which is legal and is sometimes used as a recreational drug by people who don't need it but have obtained it from those who do.

Despite these risks, is it right to deprive people of marijuana that could alleviate their suffering because someone else is going to abuse it? "Terminally ill people, disabled people, and people going blind from glaucoma are being arrested and prosecuted for using marijuana therapeutically," stated one person testifying before the DEA. "I find this situation morally repugnant."[10]

In just one decade of wrestling with the issue of using marijuana for medical purposes, over seventy thousand people have been blinded by glaucoma, hundreds of thousands more have suffered from seizures, muscle spasms, or nausea, or wasted away due to AIDS.

CHAPTER 7

Planet Earth

"Farmers in the U.S. should be free to grow whatever crop they can make a profit on," declared Lennice Werth, a candidate running for director of a county department of soil and water conservation in Virginia.[1] "Why should farmers in England, France, or New Zealand have the competitive edge?" Werth was referring to hemp—as marijuana is called when it is grown for industrial purposes. In 1996, the American Farm Bureau, the nation's largest farm organization, called hemp "one of the most promising crops in half a century."[2]

Hemp is a weed. And trying to outlaw a weed that grows nearly everywhere in the world is as difficult as outlawing nature. But in 1937, the U.S. government's Marijuana Tax Act effectively quashed the entire domestic hemp production and manufacturing industries—ending legal medical and recreational uses as well as industrial uses such as fiber, food, and paper.

During World War II, the government allowed farmers to grow hemp to meet the armed forces' need for rope and twine. When the war

Hemp Glossary

biomass: organic matter, such as plants, that can be converted to fuel and used as an energy source.

Cannabis: Latin classification for the plant that produces marijuana, hashish, and hemp fiber. Cannabis is also called ganja, hashish, pot, and marijuana.

Cannabis indica: variety of cannabis known as "skunk," which can grow anywhere in the world. (*Cannabis indica* can be crossed with *Cannabis sativa* to produce a hybrid that grows anywhere yet retains the psychotropic qualities of *sativa*.)

Cannabis sativa: variety of cannabis known for its high THC content; grows in warm, tropical climates.

hemp: common historical name for cannabis and the usual term when cannabis is used for industrial purposes, such as hemp fiber and hemp paper. Other tropical plants such as jute also produce fibers known as "hemp."

marijuana: once an obscure name for cannabis, used in a Mexican drinking song. The term marijuana came into popular usage during the 1930s' campaign to prohibit the drug.

methanol: fuel that comes from plants, such as corn, soybeans, sugarcane, and other sources of biomass.

sinsemilla: female cannabis plant that is unpollinated by the male plant. Known for its exceedingly high THC content (as much as 15 percent).

tetrahydrocannabinol (THC): the compound derived from cannabis that affects mental activity.

Marijuana plants can grow nearly anywhere in the world and, in fact, grow wild in many areas.

ended, the prohibition was renewed. In 1961 the United States signed the Single Convention Treaty on Narcotic Drugs, enacted by the United Nations. One article of the treaty allows hemp to be grown for industrial or horticultural purposes.[3] Ignoring this exemption, the United States government remains committed to a total ban on growing hemp. Recently, the ban against imported hemp has been lifted, and items such as hemp cloth, hemp oil, and hemp paper can be brought in.

Some nations allow hemp to be grown for industrial use. Farmers in Russia grow over two hundred varieties and supply 75 percent of the world's hemp. China is edging in on the market, especially for hemp paper. Hungary, England, France, Germany, and other nations allow hemp to be grown for use in textiles, paper, rope, and other products. And with good reason. This humble plant offers Planet Earth a valuable resource.

As a Crop

Cannabis is known for its THC content, the substance that produces a euphoric effect when cannabis is dried, then inhaled or ingested. THC is found in the leaves and is most concentrated in the flower of the female plant—the one that produces seeds. Some varieties of cannabis contain little or no THC and are unpleasant to smoke.

Among the more than two hundred different varieties of cannabis, *Cannabis sativa* and *Cannabis indica* are two of the most common. Although all varieties produce a significant amount of cellulose that can be spun into fiber, *Cannabis sativa* produces some of the finest hemp fiber. Most, but not all, varieties contain THC.

Cannabis is an herbaceous crop, meaning it is grown from seed each year. In addition, it is dioecious—there are two distinct sexes. The male contains flowers and a stamen that produces pollen. The female has a smaller flower and a pistil that receives the male's pollen. After fertilization with pollen, the female plant produces the seeds needed to grow new plants.

If the female fails to receive pollen, it cannot form seeds. When this occurs under controlled conditions, the plant's fruit, known as *sinsemilla* (Spanish for "without seed"), has an exceedingly high THC content.

By cross-pollinating—taking male pollen from one variety and using it to pollinate a female from a different variety—cannabis growers have created hybrids, or new varieties. Cannabis can grow up to sixteen feet (4.9 m), but some hybrids are only inches high. This allows indoor cultivation in basements and other secret places that may escape detection. Growers have also created hybrids that resemble tomato and other legal plants, again, to escape detection by drug agents.

For over ten thousand years, people have cultivated cannabis or harvested wild cannabis. The plant was used in religious ceremonies as a sacrament (to achieve euphoria) and as an herbal medicine. Its numerous other uses include fiber for rope, twine, sailcloth, clothing, and more. Its seeds were harvested for food and oil, its cellulose used for paper and plastic. According to some experts, hemp has nearly fifty thousand uses!

A Good Crop

As a crop, hemp has few insect enemies, and its dense leaves choke out weeds. Thus it requires few or no pesticides to cultivate. The plant's long roots penetrate into the soil, breaking it up and protecting it from erosion. This quality also makes hemp plants drought resistant.[4] Corn, cotton, sugarcane, and tobacco deplete the soil and rob it of nutrients. As a result, farmers need chemical fertilizers to restore nutrients to the soil. In contrast, hemp requires no fertilizing and even returns nutrients to the soil. It can help restore marginal soil to productivity, making it an ideal crop to alternate with cotton or tobacco. It can also be grown on land unsuitable for other cash crops.

Because it has a short growing period, several crops of hemp can be produced in a year—two in colder climates and four in warmer areas such as California. Hemp can be grown after other crops have been harvested, allowing farmers to earn more from their land. Hemp also outdistances other crops for productivity. One acre of hemp yields two to three times as much fiber as an acre of cotton and over four times the pulp of an acre of mature trees. As a result, hemp can reduce the amount of land now used (and sometimes destroyed) for industry and agriculture.

Some proponents claim that hemp could help curb the depletion of our ozone layer, as hemp restores ozone to the atmosphere.

Hemp is the strongest natural fiber in the world.[5] It rivals linen for durability, cotton for comfort, and wool for insulation and absorbency. It is biodegradable and environmentally safer to produce than cotton fiber.

The uses of hemp:

* *Hemp can be converted to use as fuel, replacing gasoline.*

* *Each ton of paper made from hemp would eliminate the need to cut down twelve mature trees.*

* *Hemp can be made into strong cloth, as in this wallet, and money printed on hemp would last three times as long as that printed on paper.*

As an Energy Source

Biomass—plant material that can be converted to fuel—can be used to provide energy for all sorts of engines, especially automobiles. During World War II, when petroleum was in short supply, methanol (a fuel from biomass) was used to run farm machinery and military vehicles. Today in Brazil, over a million cars run on fuel from biomass.[6] As a biomass, hemp can be converted to use as fuel, a plan once pursued by one of the pioneers of the auto industry, Henry Ford.

We are already highly dependent on foreign sources of oil. During the next century, some experts estimate that the United States will have exhausted 80 percent of its petroleum reserves. What then? Will we strip-mine for coal? Build more nuclear power plants? Go to war over petroleum? Raze our forests to make room for more corn crops for use as fuel? A large hemp crop could meet some of this energy need and decrease our reliance on foreign sources.

Fossil fuels, such as petroleum, contain sulfur. Fuels from biomass, like hemp and corn, contain no sulfur, which makes them cleaner burning fuels. Moreover, fossil fuel is not renewable, while hemp is a renewable source of fuel. Indeed, farming only 6 percent of the current agricultural land in the United States with biomass crops like hemp could fill all the gas and oil energy needs now met with fossil fuels.[7]

Tree-Free Paper

At one time hemp was widely used for paper; the original drafts of both the Declaration of Independence and the Constitution were on hemp paper, as was the nation's first paper money supply.

Paper made from wood turns yellow and brittle and deteriorates in less than a century. Paper made from hemp lasts as long as fifteen hundred years without cracking, yellowing, or crumbling, making it ideal for use in archives, books, and currency. Canada, England, and some other countries now use hemp for their paper money, which lasts three times as long as American dollars.[8]

In 1916, the federal government was concerned about dwindling timberlands and asked the Department of Agriculture to look at the problem. Lyster Dewey, a fiber expert, and Jason Merrill, a chemist, were recruited for the job. Results of their research were published in the Department of Agriculture's bulletin 404. Lyster and Merrill recommended that the government start growing hemp for fiber and paper because it made more sense than using the same land for wood-pulp production.

Currently, 93 percent of the world's paper is made from wood pulp. Yet hemp yields four times more pulp per acre than timber. This means that for every tract of ten thousand acres devoted to hemp, forty thousand acres of forest could be saved. Hemp paper can be recycled seven times, compared to three times for tree-pulp paper. Hemp does not have to be bleached with powerful chlorines that damage the water supply and release chemicals into the atmosphere.[9]

Paul Stanford, owner of a Portland, Oregon, company that manufactures paper from imported hemp, claims that half of all the trees cut down in the U.S. today are used for paper production.[10] He suggests that hemp could easily meet the current demand for paper pulp.

Other Uses

Besides industrial uses, hemp is valuable as a food source. Hemp cheese contains no cholesterol. Hemp seeds are an excellent source of protein, and hemp oil is used in Eastern medicine. Hemp can also be used to make cellophane and can be molded into many kinds of plastic.

The Ban on Hemp Begins

Why does the U.S. continue to outlaw the growth and production of hemp? Why is hemp, especially the varieties that are unsuitable for recreational use, banned as a crop?

During our nation's colonial period, hemp was legal, and growing it was encouraged. Many of the era's sailing ships caught the wind in hemp sails. The crews wore hemp breeches and shirts, shinnied up hemp ropes, and ate hemp gruel for supper. Thomas Jefferson and George Washington both cultivated hemp and advised others to follow suit.

Eventually, as cotton, tobacco, and livestock became more profitable, hemp production declined. By the 1900s, demand for hemp was largely confined to use in twine, cords, and carpet thread.

Many players contributed to the demise of the hemp industry. To begin, there was media magnate William Randolph Hearst, who reigned over a newspaper and magazine empire. Hearst favored prohibition of many substances—cigarettes and tobacco, alcohol, caffeine, cocaine, heroin, opium, and hemp. Hearst controlled vast acres of timberland, much of it in Mexico, which supplied cheap newsprint for his publications. Then, Mexican rebel Pancho Villa and his troops—many of whom smoked cannabis—seized eighty thousand acres of Hearst's timberland and returned it to Mexican peasants. Hearst sought revenge. His journalists began referring to hemp as "marijuana," after a name in a Mexican drinking song about Villa. The media war against hemp—or, marijuana—was ruthless.

Often, Hearst printed fabricated stories in his newspaper of people driven to violent crimes or insanity by marijuana use. Exaggeration, prejudice, racism, and lies colored the articles attacking marijuana users, who were often poor and members of minority groups.

Another key player with an interest in eliminating the hemp industry was multimillionaire banker Andrew Mellon, who served as U.S. secretary of the treasury for many years in the same period. Mellon had taken over the Gulf Oil Corporation and so had a personal interest in seeing that hemp lost the battle as a fuel supply for automobiles and other vehicles.

Other opponents of hemp included Mellon's millionaire friend Henry DuPont, who had inherited his family's munitions firm and was now venturing into the budding petrochemical industry. Added to this cast was Harry Angslinger, who was married to DuPont's niece and was head of the newly formed Federal Narcotics Burea, an agency within the domain of the FBI. Like Hearst, Angslinger was intent on cleansing

American society of "dope." These players worked to ban the recreational use of marijuana, citing the crime and poverty problems in the country. Crime and poverty were problems, but Angslinger's primary motives were greed and ambition.

In 1937, the nation was facing severe economic depression, political isolation following World War I, the problems arising from Prohibition, and other issues. Angslinger and his comrades quietly pushed through a bill to tax hemp, thus effectively banning it. There was little opposition as hardly anyone in the hemp industry or medical community knew about the hearings for passage of the marijuana tax, which were held by a small congressional committee. The hearings were announced as concerning "marijuana," which was still a rarely used term.

Thus, with no scientific evidence offered, no testimony from the medical community, no public hearings, and not even a congressional roll call[11]—and amid racism, scapegoating, and hysteria about marijuana and crime—marijuana was rendered illegal for all purposes.

The same year that the Marijuana Tax Act took effect—1937—the German-invented decorticator was first marketed. This machine substantially reduced the cost of processing hemp—from fifty cents to half a cent a pound.[13] *Mechanical Engineering* and *Popular Mechanics* heralded the new invention, predicting that "hemp will bring a new industry to the Corn Belt this year and provide rope for the Navy."[12]

Five years later, the United States faced a serious problem. After the Japanese bombing of Pearl Harbor and the Japanese occupation of the Philippines at the start of World War II, the supply of jute needed for rope, twine, and other military supplies was cut off. The U.S. Department of Agriculture then encouraged U.S. farmers to grow hemp, providing them with hemp seed, machines, and planting instructions. By 1943, over twenty thousand farmers were annually producing nearly sixty thousand tons (54,431 tonnes) of hemp.

With the end of the war, hemp production ended. Once more, it was a crime to grow hemp—of any variety and for any purpose.

As a crop, hemp has considerable advantages, from its suitability for marginal land to its huge product potential. A renewed hemp industry could create thousands of jobs, as well as contribute to gainingeconomic security for farmers.

Of course, as in the case of medical marijuana, the fear remains that allowing hemp to be for grown for industrial use—even if it contains only 0.3 percent THC, as the recent trade agreements such as NAFTA and GATT propose—will pave the way for allowing its recreational use, especially among adolescents. And that, claim critics, is worse than relying on petroleum imports, worse than defoliating our forests and depleting our petroleum supplies, and worse than using pesticides and fertilizers for crops and threatening the ozone layer.

CHAPTER 8

The Question of Crime

Reverend Patrick M. was an associate pastor at a New Jersey church and chaplain for the town's police and fire departments. According to his parishioners, Father Pat was a workaholic. On a typical day, observed one, "He'd visit four hospitals, see thirty-two patients, then rush back to the rectory to work on the bulletin. After that there was altar boy practice and more house calls."[1] Reverend Pat was also a cocaine user.

One day he was arrested for possession of a small amount of the drug. Shortly afterwards, at a prayer service, congregants were seen crying. "How can we help him?" they asked. "We're storming heaven with prayers to get him back," said one parishioner.

Father Pat was arrested, like anyone else who gets caught using an illicit substance. He was arrested like Patricia E., the principal of a suburban Maryland elementary school.[2] Like Father Pat, Patricia was respected by her peers but was using drugs. "There are a lot of shocked and upset people in the education community," lamented one of them.

While people in her community felt sadness for Patricia, they were outraged by her behavior. "I can't stand it that she dragged kids into all of this," said one student's mother. "Principal is the last position a drug dealer should be in." Principal is also the last position Patricia may hold for a long time. In her state, possession and intent to distribute marijuana carries a minimum sentence of twenty years in prison.

Drug reform requires a careful look at the relationship between drugs and crime: How much crime is generated by people breaking the drug laws? How much is due to the influence of drugs, fights over drug turf, or engagement in a criminal lifestyle? Only when we sort out the answers to these questions can we ask: Will a change in the drug laws give us more or less crime?

We know illicit drug use is common. Nearly two out of every five citizens has used an illicit drug in their lifetime. Among these millions of drug users and abusers are many otherwise law-abiding citizens. Yet because it is illegal to use illicit drugs, each one is guilty of breaking the law.

How Much Crime Is Due to Drug Use?

According to the federal drug laws, it is a crime to use, possess, manufacture, or distribute drugs classified as having a potential for abuse. Further, drugs contribute to other crimes. The high cost of maintaining drug habits compels addicts to steal. Certain drugs also affect people's behavior, causing them to commit violent crimes. In addition, violence is committed by dealers as they compete for drug turf. How much would these kinds of crimes decrease if drugs were legal? Or how much would they increase?

In 1996, 1.6 million citizens were arrested for drug crimes.[3] A million of these arrests were for possession of an illicit drug—nearly half for possession of marijuana. Most of the people committing the crime of distributing drugs are small-scale dealers. At least one out of ten people who use an illicit drug regularly sell small quantities of it—once a month or less often—usually to someone they know.[4] Legalizing marijuana would do away with nearly half a million arrests each year.

Given these statistics and the call from some quarters to cease jailing nonviolent drug users, it is helpful to consider this fact: Much of the crime in America is *linked* to drugs. In a survey of violent crime victims, one-third reported that they believed their assailants had been under the influence of drugs or alcohol (the drug most frequently blamed is alcohol—which is legal).[5] According to another survey, four out of five state prison inmates admitted using drugs prior to their arrest, and three out of five admitted to using drugs regularly.[6] And inmates who were using drugs committed significantly more crimes than those who were not using drugs.

According to the research of criminologist Paul Goldstein and others, the notion that drug addicts are "crazed killers" is untrue.[7] Nevertheless, a hard-core group of young people—mostly male, poor, uneducated, and from disrupted families lacking supervision—are committing much of the crime today. According to one government study, 2 percent of the people using drugs are responsible for nearly 40 percent of all thefts and assaults, some of which are quite violent.[8]

Even if they continue using drugs when they grow up (and many of them will), they will stop committing other crimes. Still, half of them are destined to become repeat adult offenders.

Drug Law Violence

Dealers who are violent criminals tend to settle their disputes violently. Beginning in the 1980s, some peaceful neighborhoods and apartment buildings became unwilling hosts to crack dealers and violent gangs. Two California gangs, the Bloods and the Crips, established drug networks through the Midwest, invading Omaha, St. Louis, Cincinnati, and other cities. Thousands of members of Jamaican gangs called "posses" were selling crack throughout the United States. They sold it cheaply, and they were armed to kill anyone who stood in their way. Observed David Boaz of the Cato Institute, a think tank, "You don't see shootouts in the car, liquor, or tobacco business. But if you have a dispute with another dealer, if he rips you off, you can't sue him, you can't take him to court, you can't do anything except use violence."[9]

Dealers are showing greater resourcefulness than ever. They are abandoning their former "open-air bazaars" for sophisticated indoor operations. Today's drug dealers use one apartment for selling drugs, another for storing them, and still another for stashing away their profits.[10] Their cars are customized, so that the push of a hidden button opens a secret dashboard compartment. Yet the fight over drug turf continues. Explained a New York gang member, who was being secretly videotaped by police: "We sell drugs and we kill."

This kind of violence might be lessened if drugs were legal or at least regulated by the government. On the other hand, in cities such as New York, which have gotten tougher on drug crime, drug-related homicides have dropped substantially without any reform in the drug laws.

Because drug crime is rampant, many city dwellers are fearful in their own neighborhoods, regardless of the time of day. That's because drugs are sold around the clock. Walter M. lives in a home that was once safe. "You could keep your door unlocked," he recalled. "Now, I lock it even when I'm in my yard and can watch it. My dining room faces the street. I don't sit in there at night anymore with the lights on. There's too much shooting around here. Our biggest fear is getting hit by a stray bullet."[11]

For years, police have encouraged citizens to help fight crime in their own neighborhoods. They urge them to form neighborhood watches and to report crimes, identify suspects, and testify against them. Herman Wrice teaches ordinary citizens to fight drug dealers through direct, non-violent confrontation, a method of defense he has taught in more than 350 communities throughout the United States. Protest marchers pick a drug dealer's house or corner and disrupt sales through relentless jeering and taunting. Sometimes off-duty police join the groups.[12]

But in the opinion of Lawrence W. Sherman, a criminologist at the University of Maryland, it is too much to ask private citizens to enlist in the fight against drugs. He says, "We should not urge citizen volunteers to fight the war on drugs alone. Not even Smokey the Bear wants us to rush into forest fires with a garden hose." Despite the risks, a few brave citizens try anyway.

Maria and her husband, Carlos, had three children. The youngest was only three. When crack dealers infested their neighborhood in Brooklyn, New York, the couple chased them from the apartment building they owned. Although Carlos was shot twice by drug dealers and stabbed by a neighbor he had accused of drug dealing, the couple persisted. Both fed police information about local drug dealers. Then, one morning, drug dealers fired a spray of bullets through the bedroom window. A bullet hit Maria in the temple and killed her.

Drug Use and Criminal Behavior

Most adults who use drugs do not commit crimes other than possession of an illegal substance. It is young people, particularly those who have acquired a heroin, crack cocaine, or other hard-drug habit, who commit most drug-related crime. As drug users age, most who had been committing crimes stop (or they die, often violently or of an overdose, or are in jail). What the aging hard-core users do, though, is continue to create a market for illegal drugs.[13]

Legalization would not stop all the crime associated with drugs. Alcohol is legal. Yet many alcoholics abuse their families, drive recklessly, rape, rob, and murder. The same kinds of crimes occur when people abuse certain drugs, particularly stimulants, barbiturates, and PCP, which can cause users to anger quickly and lose control of their aggression.[14]

Certain general tendencies in drug-related crime can be noted. Crimes such as theft are more likely to be committed by regular users of cocaine and heroin than by people using marijuana. Criminologist Paul Goldstein suggests that violence attributed to marijuana and heroin can be largely discredited because marijuana and heroin can actually "ameliorate" violent tendencies.

On the other hand, if drug law repeal paves the way to greater use of drugs like PCP, which causes some users to be extremely violent, it could be responsible for many more tragedies.

Committing Crime to Pay for Drugs

According to FBI data, the link between crime and drugs is significant. For example, one-third of all thefts are committed to get money to buy high-priced drugs such as cocaine and heroin. In fact, many addicts become so desperate for drugs that they will resort to any means to get money. For drugs or drug money, some people sell their bodies for sex, deal drugs, steal, even kill. For many, vice and crime are constant companions. One crack-dependent mother was arrested and charged with trying to sell her eleven-year-old daughter to a rapist in order to get money for a drug habit.

To sustain a two-hundred-dollar-a-day habit, an addict needs to steal at least one thousand dollars' worth of goods a day.[15] Many steal far more than that. The average drug addict relying on theft for drug money will commit three hundred crimes a year.

To support a heroin or cocaine habit, some addicts resort to crime or prostitution.

A great deal of the property crime in the United States is committed by drug users in search of cash or goods to support their habits. This translates to 4 million thefts a year—$7.5 billion in stolen property,[16] an amount just half of what the federal government spent fighting drugs in 1996. How much crime could be avoided if drugs were legal and affordable?

Bribery and Corruption

Occasionally, public servants find themselves on the wrong side of the struggle. On January 18, 1990, the FBI videotaped Marion Barry, mayor of the District of Columbia, smoking crack cocaine.[17] In 1994, nine New

Orleans police officers were indicted for accepting nearly one hundred thousand dollars in bribes to protect a drug-trafficking ring; another twenty officers were implicated.[18]

Human nature being what it is, combined with the enormous amount of money involved in illegal drug trading—$50 billion a year in the U.S.—some law enforcement officers whose job is to catch criminals catch the greed of drug-money fever instead.

As one example, a twenty-year veteran of the DEA was recently arrested on drug-smuggling charges. Along with his two brothers, Edward O'Brien was arrested at Logan International Airport in Boston when he tried to deliver sixty-two pounds (28 kg) of cocaine to an undercover informant. The irony of O'Brien's arrest is that in 1973 he had helped to close the "French Connection" case, which broke up a major heroin importing ring. Commented John J. Coleman Jr., one of O'Brien's friends and head of the Boston DEA office, "Of my hundreds of arrests in my career, this will always be the toughest. Greed can cloud the judgment of the best of us."[19]

Greed clouded the judgment of three former DEA agents charged with laundering more than $608,000 in drug money through Swiss banks. The U.S. attorney general blamed their conduct on the "corrupting effects of drug trafficking." If drugs were legal, this kind of temptation would be removed.

Criminals and Drugs

For most drug offenders, buying, using, and selling small amounts of marijuana is their only crime. Legalizing marijuana would take the crime out of using it (although not any of the risks). It could also keep those who use it from getting involved with a criminal element and people likely to push them into harder drugs or cause them harm.

Jennifer paid a high price for her involvement with drugs. At seventeen, she seemed a clean-cut, well-behaved high school student living in the Pocono Mountains of Pennsylvania. On June 29, 1995, she asked a friend to come with her to meet the teenage drug dealer who had been her cocaine supplier. She owed him four hundred dollars. When he arrived, he shot and killed both young women, then fled.

Some sociologists believe that a small segment of the population finds excitement in breaking the law, challenging authority, and defying society's rules. Members of this "culture of crime" are attracted to illicit drugs precisely because they are illegal. For the same reasons that they are attracted to drugs, they are attracted to crime. Thus, changing the drug laws may dissuade them from entering the drug trade. It may stop their violent drug turf battles. Because they are already drawn to violence and crime, however, no matter what the drug laws are, they will remain a threat to society.

According to criminologist Paul Goldstein, each year more than 350,000 years of life are lost to drug-related homicides, and more than 250,000 days of hospital care are required for victims of drug-related assaults.[20] Governmental regulation of hard drugs like heroin would give those who steal and commit violent crimes to support their habits less incentive to do so.

While a change in drug laws may change certain behavior, it will not change all behavior. Some people will still be drawn to criminal organizations and to gangs and will still engage in crime, misuse drugs, or use drugs that cause them to be violent, irresponsible, or abusive toward others. If drugs like PCP, anabolic steroids, and amphetamines were legal, that kind of behavior might well increase.

CHAPTER 9

Risky Business

The American Dream: Get Rich and Live Happily Ever After

With their good looks, intelligence, and outgoing personalities, William and Brett Brinton had a jump start on success.[1] After they graduated from college, they founded their own computer company, B & B Software Engineering. Two years later, an explosion at B & B blew away the door and shook the entire block. It also blew away their cover when authorities searched through the wreckage and found a full-scale methamphetamine lab. The amount of ephedrine (a chemical used to manufacture amphetamines) found was enough to have grossed the brothers more than ten million dollars—enough so that the Brinton brothers had to watch the American Dream fade to the American School of Criminal Justice.

Illegal drugs earn cash—cash few teenagers can earn by other means. Teenager Tasha Moore was earning thousands of dollars a week selling drugs. "I was making so much money," Moore claims, "that when I put it in this big bag, I used to just sit there and take pictures. . . all kinds of pictures of me holding all this money." With her money Tasha purchased two cars, went to expensive clubs, and treated herself and her girlfriends to a vacation at Disneyland. "I had so much [money]," Tasha exclaims, "it was like I won the lottery. It was like that."[2]

Twice each year, Ken pays $50,000 cash for ten pounds (4.5 kg) of top-grade marijuana.[3] Afterwards he sells it to people he knows in the Los Angeles area, people who spend as much for a month's supply of grass as others pay for their home mortgage. For Kenny, it's a risky business, but one that brings in $2 million a year. Just carrying the amount of money he takes in is difficult, as it comes in small denominations—five-, ten-, and twenty-dollar bills. And a million dollars in twenty-dollar bills weighs a hundred pounds![4] To launder his drug money through a South American bank, Ken embarked on a cruise through the Panama Canal, carrying a million dollars in cash in his baggage.

Between $200 million to $300 million changes hands in the United States every single day in drug deals. In one operation, drug dealers tried to launder half a billion dollars in a single bank transaction.[5]

In 1996, the federal government alone spent over $15 billion fighting drug use. Two-thirds was spent on enforcement, the rest on treatment and prevention. Adding state and local efforts, the tab goes to $30 *billion* dollars—a gargantuan amount, but hardly enough to match the estimated $49 billion illegally earned in drugs. Marijuana crops alone bring in over $20 billion—the largest cash crop in the United States, trailed by corn, soybeans, hay, wheat, cotton, and tobacco.[6]

Cost of the War on Drugs

Money is a major issue to those who want to totally legalize drugs. Conservative economist Milton Friedman summed up the issue when he stated frankly, "The war on drugs is too expensive." Legalization, he believes, makes economic sense.

The billions now spent enforcing the drug laws could be saved if drugs were legalized. First, catching drug criminals requires human resources and equipment. Police frequently spend days on end sitting in their patrol cars, observing the comings and goings of suspects before they have enough evidence for searches or arrests. The growing number of convicted drug criminals is aggravating an already acute shortage of jails. Keeping a person in prison for one year costs the public between $16,000 and $20,000. By the turn of the century, California will need to build at least fifteen new prisons, at a cost of $4.5 billion. And the state will still have severely overcrowded prison conditions.[7]

It may be worth our tax dollars to catch big-time dealers, drug runners, and those who sell drugs to minors. But is it worth the $7 billion the government spends each year enforcing marijuana laws? At a time when the state and federal governments are trying

Consider this:

- Federal taxpayers spend nearly four times as much to incarcerate one inmate ($20,804) as to educate one child ($5,421).

- The Department of Justice's budget has grown 162 percent since enactment of mandatory minimum sentences in 1987; the budget of the Department of Education has increased only 77percent.

- Four years in prison costs more than four years at a private university (including tuition, fees, room, board, books, and supplies).

- States spend 6.4 percent of their budgets on criminal justice programs and only 3.8 percent on housing and the environment.

Source: FAMM

to balance their budgets, such spending squeezes other areas, leading to cuts in education, school lunch programs, and other essential items.

Drug Laws Make Money for Those Who Enforce Them

The billions spent fighting drug crime pays the salaries of hundreds of thousands of people, from high-level DEA agents to prison guards and parole officers. Building new jail cells to house the increased numbers of drug crime inmates provides income for tens of thousands of building contractors, construction workers, and suppliers. To build one new jail cell costs between $50,000 and $150,000,[8] while the cost of a new 1,200-cell prison runs $30 million or more. In addition, drug law enforcement, which includes state, local, and federal enforcement agents, employs over five hundred thousand full-time officers.

People wonder why police go after someone with a few marijuana plants, but such arrests may allow them to seize the entire house or the property where the plants are grown. The arrest is less dangerous than busting a cocaine or heroin drug ring and is lucrative enough to justify the effort. Money seized is divided up between various law enforcement agencies, courts, and prosecutors, and other assets may be auctioned off or used by arresting agents in future drug stings.

Justice Department forfeiture chief Cary Copeland sees forfeiture as an effective weapon against drugs. "It is to the drug war," he claims, "what smart bombs and air power are to modern warfare. It gives us the power to take out the drug kingpin by wiping out his assets."[9]

Opponents of the drug laws criticize the law that permits drug enforcement agents to seize any property used in a drug deal or suspected of being purchased with drug money. They claim that this law is abused and that people are unfairly punished. In addition, it presents a conflict of interest, since seized money and assets frequently go directly toward paying the salaries of those making the seizures.

In a five-year period, seizures in cash and property gave federal, state, and local police over a billion dollars.[10] By randomly stopping motorists on Interstate 95 in Florida, one county sheriff's department seized $5 million in cash in a year. In fact, one day's work by one officer resulted in seizures amounting to over $300.000.[11]

Today, even informants may reap windfalls. In some districts, they are entitled to keep up to 25 percent of the forfeiture profits in return for tipping off agents. In 1995, in Colombia, DEA agents paid $1.5 million for information leading to the arrest of five drug lords. "This is an investment with a tremendous return," reasons one DEA agent. "They're in it for greed, so we go after that greed."[12]

Legalized Drugs Generate Income

When liquor and cigarettes are sold, they're taxed, and the public benefits from those taxes. In contrast, drug laws deprive the public of taxes from drug sales, since drugs are illegal.

If drugs are legalized, predicts Lester Grinspoon and others, more than $10 billion in tax revenues could be collected from drug sales, revenues that could be spent on treatment and prevention programs. Taxes on marijuana alone would amount to $4–6 billion, even if many people would grow their own pot and avoid taxation.[13]

To hit dealers for unpaid taxes, Arizona passed a law requiring a Cannabis and Controlled Substances Dealer's License in 1983. Dealers were to pay the state one hundred dollars for an annual license to sell marijuana, and a tax of 10 percent of the street price. Naturally, no one bought a license or paid taxes, since selling marijuana is illegal. But then, in 1990, an engineer and frequent pot smoker bought a license and a sheet of tax stamps. By 1996, a few hundred licenses had been issued.[14] If the Arizona referendum to legalize medical marijuana had prevailed, those tax revenues would have increased even more.

Legalizing drugs will also create jobs. The Netherlands, for example, has hundreds of cannabis cafes that employ thousands of people. In an analysis of the economics of legalizing cannabis, Dale Gieringer estimates that similar cafes throughout the United States, which has a far

Taxes on sales of the legal (but lethal) drug, tobacco, provide enormous government revenues.

larger population, could involve sixty thousand retailers (owners of the cafes) and at least one hundred thousand jobs.[15] It is hard to know whether this is a realistic estimate. Still, legalization could surely create new financial opportunities.

The Downside Costs

If drugs were legalized, some experts believe that the number of drug users would increase. Even if it doesn't, the current cost of drug use in the workplace—lost productivity, absenteeism, accidents, and the like—is estimated to be over $60 billion a year. General Motors estimated that drug use among employees added costs of $150 to $200 to each car produced.[16]

Another problem would be the cost of new addicts and the cost of prevention programs. Many addicts require lengthy or repeated treatment, so if addiction increased substantially the bill for the new addicts could be staggering. Legalizing marijuana would send a message of tolerance, so new prevention programs would be needed. Better prevention programs are probably needed anyway, given how many young people are unaffected by them.

Who Will Shoulder These Costs?

If drugs were taxed to cover the cost of treatment and prevention, their prices would rise. Too high a price could encourage a new black market in even cheaper drugs to emerge. Or high prices would drive users to cheaper, and possibly more dangerous, drugs. Finally, high taxation and drug prices defeat one of the reasons for legalizing drugs in the first place—to make them affordable so users don't have to steal or deal for them.

Tax revenues cannot begin to cover the cost in human misery of drug abuse. In recent studies, researchers learned that 10 percent of pregnant women are using illegal drugs during their pregnancy, risking the health of their newborns. In areas where drugs are rampant,

An indoor marijuana operation in a Florida home

the rate is even higher. One study found that 20 percent of the pregnant women used cocaine.[17]

Babies born to these mothers are frequently premature. Many suffer withdrawal from drugs at birth, as well as lifelong damage to their physical and psychological health and their learning abilities. While such suffering has no dollar measurement, the babies' medical care does. It costs between $100,000 and $150,000 to care for a baby who is born prematurely because of crack.[18]

The High Cost of Business

Why should $4 worth of cocaine in a foreign market suddenly cost $80 on the street in the United States?

In 1995 in Myanmar (formerly Burma), a kilogram—2.2 pounds—of heroin sold for $700. After it had been transported to Thailand for refining, the same amount sold for $10,000. When a kilogram of refined heroin reaches the streets of New York City and is cut down and diluted, it can fetch *$750,000.*[19]

Consider marijuana, a crop that yields Americans over $10 billion a year in profits. For an investment of $3,000 to purchase seeds, a few hundred dollars' worth of soil, another $300 to set up a "grow" closet with lights, fans, and an irrigation system, and somewhat high electrical costs, a person can produce a crop of one hundred marijuana plants, grown on an area the size of a breakfast table. For this investment of about $10,000, someone willing to take the risk can collect $500,000 in just one harvest.[20] And a grower can produce several harvests a year. One high-grade marijuana plant can return $2,000 to $6,000 to its grower in a year. Few services or products rival this kind of profitability.

The large increase is due, in part, to the "crime tariff." This is the amount each seller adds along the way to the cost of the illegal goods to make it worth the risks involved—steep risks at that. In most states, getting caught with over a hundred marijuana plants means a minimum sentence of five years in prison, with no chance of parole. In Oklahoma, it can bring a life sentence with no parole. Selling drugs is also dangerous because of battles over turf (on the average, three drug dealers are murdered each day in the U.S.).

Legal drugs would not be risky to sell and would therefore carry no crime tariff. If they were legal, they would probably be about as profitable as alcohol or cigarettes are now. When alcohol was legalized, it was no longer profitable for organized crime to sell it, and criminals left the business. Legalizing drugs would probably have the same effect, driving the illegitimate producers and dealers out of business.

Coca leaves for sale at a street market in Bolivia

However, as legalized gambling (state lotteries) has shown, criminals may find resourceful ways to compete with legitimate business. By increasing the odds or filling special niches, they stay in the business, and stay in it *illegally*. It is doubtful that every drug lord would let legalization pave the way to retirement.

Drug Laws Keep the Price Out of Reach

A major goal of drug enforcement is to reduce the supply of illicit drugs on the streets. Drug enforcement officials often measure their success by street prices. A very high price deters people from buying drugs, because they don't have the money or are unwilling to pay so much.

During the 1980s, government agencies were so successful in cutting the heroin supply that it became expensive and difficult to buy. This probably contributed to stemming that period's heroin epidemic—though it still left nearly half a million people addicted. Unfortunately, crackdowns can backfire. Drugs can become so expensive and difficult to obtain that users turn to less expensive substitutes. These may be more dangerous and addictive than the original drugs.

Another problem with high prices is that customers want more "kick" for their money. They want stronger drugs. Although the 1980s' crack epidemic was largely the result of a widespread surplus of cocaine, some experts also blame the high price of marijuana. When law enforcement drove up the price of marijuana, many drug users, particularly those in the ghetto, turned to crack cocaine because it was cheaper and more available.

When the market is glutted with illegal drugs, prices drop. When prices drop, more people can afford to buy drugs. As more people buy them, the demand increases. Suppliers try to meet that demand and produce more drugs. Thus, while legalization may reduce the price of drugs, it does little to reduce the demand, and in fact, may even increase it. This is an economic gamble few Americans want to risk.

Many drug dealers were crooks before they started dealing drugs. Others became used to the fast dollars and lifestyle and—if drugs were legal—would probably look for other black-market activities. Or they might find new ways to exploit the old markets, such as selling drugs to minors or designing new drugs to sell outside the legal market.

Legalization would cut the billion-dollar law enforcement bill (and put many people employed through it out of work) and ease the burden on our justice system. Millions of dollars from tax revenues could be used for treatment and prevention. However, given the cost of treatment as well as the cost of drug use in general—from crack-dependent babies to lost production—most experts agree that tax revenues would be offset by these expenses.

Some costs are immeasurable. A purely economic approach to the drug war ignores the other side of the issue—the human side. Dollars gained from legalizing drugs, especially the most addictive ones, could not balance out the misery and loss of human potential.

We have already spent billions of dollars on the drug war. Perhaps we have not spent enough to succeed, or maybe we are not spending it wisely. Perhaps we should have continued to fund the war on poverty or spent more on treatment.

CHAPTER 10

Through a Glass Darkly

In the movie *Pulp Fiction*, a young woman overdoses on illegal drugs. As her character starts to foam at the mouth and bleed from the nose, some viewers recoil in disgust. Yet for many people, such scenes are common.

When police raided a Philadelphia home, they found crack vials, rolling papers, lighters, matchbooks, and bags of marijuana.[1] The kitchen contained no stove; the refrigerator held no food. The family's only toilet was backed up with excrement. Amid the litter sat two small children. Their father had abandoned them and their mother was addicted to crack cocaine. Even their grandfather sold and used drugs.

Thousands of children grow up in similar neglect, filth, abuse, and poverty. Over two hundred thousand babies are born each year to women using illegal drugs. Many of these babies are born addicted to crack and heroin.[2] Some babies die at birth; others survive to face lives with serious physical and mental problems.

Teenagers from homes ripped by drugs may find themselves heads of their households. As one such teen who turned to drug dealing said, "If there's nothing to eat at night, who's going to buy something to make sure something is there? I was the only man in the house, and they [three younger sisters] had to eat. They knew I was out there hustling for us."[3]

Many children live in deplorable conditions, failed by agencies whose assigned role is to protect them. The equation is simple but tragic: Too few caseworkers and foster homes available for the many children who need them. "We tolerate increasing levels of risk," admits the head of a support center for child advocates. "For every new user [of crack], there's a family of children who are being abused or neglected. . . . That tells me we're not winning this war when it comes to kids."[4]

Not all parents who deal or use drugs are abusive to their children. Yet far too many are. Even parents who don't use drugs find it difficult to shield their children from the turmoil and violence of the surrounding hard-drug culture.

We know that hard-drug use often leads to human misery. Not surprisingly, then, the substantial increase in the last decades in hard-drug use has brought an increase in human misery.

Elliott Currie, author of *Reckoning,* a book about the relationship between poverty, crime, and drug use in our cities, believes the war on drugs has two fronts—one among the haves and the other, a fiercer war, among the have-nots. With convincing evidence, Currie reasons that despite all our efforts to fight drug abuse, the drug scourge among our inner-city poor has, to date, been gaining ground, and for what he suggests are rather obvious reasons. Until we recognize the connection between the roots of drug abuse and the roots of poverty, concludes Currie, we will never alleviate either problem—and we will be compelled to watch the cancer in our cities spread deeper and wider.

Basically, the core problem is not that people are using or abusing drugs, or committing crimes in order to do so. Rather, it is that too many urban poor cannot participate in the American dream. More and more

Crack can invade and poison a neighborhood atmosphere. Here youths inspect crack graffitti at an inner-city open-air drug market.

of them are shut out of the dream, with little hope or resources with which to alter their fate. Subsequently, many, particularly the young, enter into a street drug culture that seems to offer them an exciting alternative, an opportunity to use their wiles, courage, and other skills that in different circumstances might have been devoted to gaining success in mainstream America.

The situation is complicated, but it is also comprehensible. From studies in the 1950s and 1960s, the tidal wave of drug abuse, as well as that of crime, despair, hopelessness, massive unemployment, dead-end jobs, and the host of other problems among the urban poor could easily have been predicted.

In 1960, President Lyndon Johnson initiated the War on Poverty. It had limited success and was gradually abandoned during the turmoil of the Vietnam War years and the 1970s and 1980s. Had it succeeded, even partially, it might have eliminated the need for a war on drugs. To succeed in a war on drugs requires more than merely fighting drug supplies, distribution, and possession—it requires a renewed war against poverty, against unemployment, homelessness, and crime.

To understand why the battlefield for a war on drugs is so large, we need to understand why drug use, in particular use of heroin, crack cocaine, and other hard drugs, reached epidemic levels during the 1980s. We also need to recognize the reasons they remain, despite a slight decline in the use of crack cocaine, a scourge on life in the city. We talk about a war on drugs and about the fight against hard drugs and addiction. In reality, though, this struggle is against *ordinary citizens who use drugs*. Even drug *use* is frequently defined as drug abuse, as though all people are incapable of using drugs in a responsible way.

The current struggle is primarily a war against the poor who use drugs. It is also a war rife with racism, as police routinely search—and bust—a disproportionate number of black and Hispanic males. Sure, whites are also subjected to drug searches and random drug tests— especially if they sport provocative bumper stickers or T-shirts. Nor does growing up in a middle- or upper-class family keep people from abusing drugs. Still, the hottest war zones are not found in the suburbs, but rather where the poor and the underprivileged dwell.

Drug Use and Abuse

Many people, liberals and conservatives alike, who are far removed from the true drug battlegrounds, see drug addiction as a medical, moral, or criminal problem. Conservatives tend to believe that the "solution" to the drug problem is to "get tough on crime"—lock up users, abusers, and dealers. Others pin their hopes on drug treatment, believing that it can get people to stop using drugs. A few see legalizing drugs as the way out of the situation.

Some criminologists believe that drug use among the poor or near poor is actually a social problem, a situation deeply embedded in the culture of poverty. Neither treatment nor punishment alone can make it go away. Only if we can resolve the root causes—the poverty and the lack of hope among our poor and near poor—can we *begin* to resolve the drug problem. Over forty years of social science research points to this conclusion, but many people fail to look at the issue from this vantage point. And their failure has led to serious flaws and short-comings in our local and national drug policies.

Some people point a finger of blame at the drug addicts, at mothers using crack whose babies are born addicted, or at addicted men and women sharing needles and passing on infections. Others blame the situation on the greed of drug dealers, the ruthlessness of drug gangs, and the racism of our society.

And we ask, which comes first: poverty and crime, or drugs? Can we ever solve one problem without solving the other? Indeed, are there *any* resolutions to such monumental problems?

The first question to ask, though, is why drugs are such a magnet. Why don't more people travel the conventional road of hard work and sustain their hope in the American dream?

The Lure of Drugs

People use drugs for many reasons:

Cool cat. Many hard-drug users don't fit the down-and-out stereotype. Instead, they are the "cool cats" running the show. Because illicit drugs pose danger and risk, some urban men see hard-drug use and dealing in hard drugs as a way to earn status and self-esteem, even though the rewards may be temporary and cost them their lives.

Malcolm X wrote in his autobiography that when he was first introduced to drugs and entered a social circle of people doing drugs, he believed he had gained status and money. Other young black males

117

have followed that path. With their prospects for entering mainstream America dim, they embark on the fast track of hard drugs, crime, and high living. They see people around them on drugs and getting rich.

Escape from reality. For many people, including young, single women, drugs seem to offer an escape from the stress of living in squalor, crime, and despair. According to a 1994 survey, one in four mothers on welfare used illicit drugs or alcohol excessively.[5] This translates to over a million women. Among the youngest, the rate goes up to one out of three. Another study revealed that 80 percent of all children in foster homes have a parent who abuses drugs.[6]

Surrounded by drugs. Some people do drugs because many people around them are using them. Their society seems a "culture of drugs." And in a drug culture, participation is "normal." Drugs provide structure to their lives—albeit a structure with no long-term rewards. The routine of hustling and using drugs takes over their days, and escape is difficult.

Like the "cool cat" motive, participating in the drug culture gives poor people a chance to participate in American consumerism. They want the material goods and luxury that drug money can buy. "When I see a kid my age driving a Mercedes," concedes a sixteen-year-old serving a prison term for selling crack cocaine, "I want the same thing. It's not easy to quit. The environment I live in is nothing but drugs."[7]

Young children copy the grown-ups they see. When adults in their lives do drugs, they want to try them, too. "I've seen guys like eleven years old selling drugs," explained one young dealer. "If they see their brother selling it, they want to be like their brother."[8]

For many, drugs seem to be everywhere. As a Brooklyn teenager trying to stay clean after breaking away from heroin and crack said, "Everywhere I go, drugs are there. And I want to use them. Sometimes my mind says, 'Get high, get high.' It's real hard. I know how good it feels in the beginning. But I know the consequences."[9]

Resisting drugs in a culture where they are entrenched is difficult. In some cities, such as East Detroit, drugs create ghettos of crime and

Some turn to drugs for an escape from overwhelmingly difficult reality.

abuse, where the culture of drugs is deeply intertwined with the culture of poverty. So tangled is the connection that, according to Currie and other experts, neither education, individual drug treatment, nor the threat of arrest and prison—the traditional weapons used in the fight against drugs—can ever cure the problems.

Maelstroms in the Making

Decades ago, the urban poor often could find support from extended families—grandparents, aunts, uncles, and cousins who helped each other succeed and create better lives. Through churches and community organizations, neighborhoods could give a person valuable support and a sense of belonging. But these support networks have all but disappeared for many of the urban poor. Many forces contributed to the destruction of both family and neighborhood support. Some experts cite the effects of the 1960s' race riots. Later, in a quest for urban renewal, expressways cut through some neighborhoods and the demolition ball leveled others, displacing people into crowded, impersonal public housing projects.

As movie theaters, grocery stores, and other establishments went bankrupt, closed, or were relocated to safer areas, local economies suffered. The absence of these establishments created everyday hardships for the communities. Public funding for the War on Poverty dried up, leaving people homeless, transient, and without ambulances, fire stations, libraries, school supplies, and other essentials.

At the same time, a change in the job market caused economic disaster for many individuals, families, and neighborhoods. Earlier, people with a high school education or less could earn decent wages in blue-collar (manual labor), clerical, and other work. When businesses and large employers left the cities, jobs went with them. During the 1980s, Detroit lost one hundred thousand jobs; New York City ninety-five thousand.[10] True, other jobs opened up. But with little education and no means to travel to these jobs—many of which were relocated from the city to the suburbs—the urban poor could not gain access to them.

People advocating welfare reform, such as those in favor of the Contract with America, have admonished welfare recipients to get jobs and get off the dole. Yet jobs elude many. Unemployment runs high in the ghetto—nearly one out of five adults who want work cannot find a job. And the competition is fierce, even for low-paying, menial jobs. In East Harlem, for example, for every applicant who lands a job, thirteen will be rejected.[11]

Jobs that are available offer little or no financial security. A job paying six dollars an hour will fail to raise a family above the poverty line. Many jobs pay less than that. Moreover, for poor mothers facing sixty to seventy dollars in weekly child-care costs, the prospects of climbing out of poverty look dim.

Nor does the new job sector offer decent benefits or opportunity for advancement or personal fulfillment. In short, large numbers of urban poor have grown up unemployed and remain unemployed. Increasingly, when they do find work, their poor-paying, dead-end jobs give them no hope of improving their skills or moving into better jobs.

This dismal job market and economy have caused major housing problems. Elliott Currie describes one of the poorest black neighborhoods he has seen:

> The level of urban devastation approaches the surreal; it does not get much worse than this anywhere in the United States. Virtually every block has its abandoned and plywooded homes, some in the early stages of collapse. . . . In front of a few homes, people are selling their furniture: they're moving, they've been evicted, or they need the money to buy crack cocaine.
>
> Old mattresses, decrepit overstuffed chairs, and various odds and ends clutter the front yards; clothes for sale are displayed forlornly across weathered porches. Stripped and demolished cars, trucks, and old buses dot the side streets and litter the vacant lots.[12]

As Currie's description points out, good housing is in short supply. Federally funded housing, once a glimmer of hope on the horizon, does not come close to meeting the current demand. As a result, thousands of people are homeless and thousands more are constantly moving, which disrupts family life and community support.

For these reasons—joblessness, dead-end work, lack of family and

*Abandoned homes and closed-up businesses line the streets
of devastated urban neighborhoods.*

community help, and many more as well—our urban poor and near
poor grow poorer decade by decade. Impoverished in the pocket and
impoverished in spirit, drug use and abuse sustains its grip.

Closing the Gap

Only by closing the increasingly wide gap between the haves and have-
nots, only by lifting people out of poverty and improving the quality
of their family life, housing, schools, and neighborhoods, and by offering them hope as well, can we begin to wage a successful battle against
drug use and abuse.

This is a tall order for any society and, interestingly, an especially challenging one for an industrial nation. With the exception of such poor nations as Afghanistan and Nigeria, which are drug suppliers, not a single industrial nation faces the level of drug abuse that exists in the United States.[13] Nor does any other industrial nation have the level of poverty that exists among our urban poor. To overcome poverty and crime requires a massive human effort and money and commitment; so, too, does the rebuilding of neighborhoods, family life, schools, fire stations, and other resources.

Currie suggests that while many solutions sound idealistic, they may be feasible—but expensive—and require a Herculean effort. Currie proposes using incentive programs to entice businesses and employers back into the inner city so people can earn decent wages, which in turn can take them off the drug-infested streets in their neighborhoods. He would also like to raise the minimum wage enough to allow working teenagers and parents to rebuild family life.

We gave up on the War on Poverty too soon. Victory might have eluded us, but had we secured it, much of the crime, violence, and hard drug use and addiction now eroding the quality of life in our cities might have been prevented.

Until we undertake a massive fight against poverty, victory against drug abuse will elude us—no matter how many drug arrests we make or how many jails we construct, no matter how many police or drug counselors we hire. Furthermore, our cities' problems are so terrible, they blemish the fabric of our society and threaten to rip apart the seams of life everywhere. In an age of mobility and instant communication, there is little escape from crime or the fear of crime. When one segment of society suffers, the entire society suffers.

Many people see little of the lives of the desperately poor. They question the value of directing tax dollars to fight another war on poverty. Instead, they wish to deal directly with the drug problem. However, legalizing drugs through total repeal of all drug laws could exacerbate the situation. With despair coursing through people's lives, drugs, legal or otherwise, seem to promise an escape—however temporary—from stress and responsibility. Legalized drugs might offer an even easier, less expensive escape—much the way cheap alcohol does. On the other hand, decriminalizing certain drugs, such as marijuana, could destroy some of their glamour, as it has in the Netherlands. And allowing addicts to supply their habits without resorting to burglary and other serious crimes could alleviate some of the violence and crime in the city. Still, such solutions only skim the surface of despair, and some may intensify the problems.

Whether or not drugs are legalized or decriminalized seems to lose significance beside the larger social ills—especially unemployment, homelessness, and lack of hope among our nation's poor. And a combined war on drugs and poverty might cost the public more than any war they have ever fought. Yet it could be our most just war.

The Flip Side

It is important to put the problems of the cities in perspective. Many people struggle to keep their family life strong and good, and people *do* succeed in rising above poverty.

Stricter gun control can decrease the incidence of murder and violent crime. If cities had more funds for tearing down the abandoned buildings that drug dealers use, or if they offered greater financial incentives for restoring these buildings, open drug dealing might be out of reach—and out of sight—of children and teenagers. Certainly, the programs that have succeeded on these fronts should create optimism.

Nor can drugs be blamed for all the problems, either in the cities or among those privileged enough to be living the American dream. Scientists, writers, and others who have achieved professional and financial success have occasionally used drugs and some have kept drugs from ruining their lives. Yet far too many people have destroyed their creative potential or tragically ended their lives because of dependence on drugs. While other factors contribute, when young, talented people like actor River Phoenix die of an overdose, many people question whether drugs should be legalized. How many of those who avoid drugs and drug addiction *because* drugs are illegal would suffer River Phoenix's fate if drugs were legal?

On the other hand, perhaps neither drug laws nor their repeal could have saved rock star Curt Cobain or River Phoenix from their heroin habits or their early deaths.

The world has many problems that neither drugs nor drug reform can solve. We must learn to recognize when drugs have a *connection* to these problems and when our drug policy actually *causes* those problems.

Poverty and human misery never justify harmful behavior. Yet they *can* explain it. When policymakers understand this, and perhaps exercise empathy with those people, they will use more appropriate weapons in their fight against drugs. But most importantly, it behooves us all to do something to make a better place for those people who peer through the glass of their lives darkly.

CHAPTER 11

A Foreign Affair

In the Chapare jungle of Bolivia lies a region that produces nearly a third of the world's supply of coca. Deep in the jungle is a secret airstrip where planes on clandestine missions drop off drug money and processing chemicals and load up with coca base, all in a matter of minutes.

It is dawn on day sixty-six of mission "Ghost Zone." U.S. Customs agents detect two aircraft sneaking in from opposite directions. Although the drug planes can accomplish their mission within minutes, a fog prevents them from taking off. Outside the operations center, other drug agents wait for the "snowcaps"—Bolivians who have been trained by the U.S. to combat drugs. "We are at war," explains the DEA chief assigned to Bolivia.[1] Setting up the base camp and supplying Ghost Zone's twenty-three outposts with fuel, aircraft, vehicles, ships, chase boats, and other necessary equipment is a huge task.

Suddenly the fog lifts. Two U.S. soldiers and six Bolivians climb into helicopters. One drug plane has already lifted off and eluded capture.

Before they can go after the other plane, the troops are called back to base. Apparently, seven dealers have been located in the jungle and are in a shoot-out with drug agents. To end the shoot-out, six choppers with about sixty soldiers take off. Trucks will transport another sixty. Unfortunately, after three hours of travel over rough and bumpy roads, the group arrives to find that the Colombian drug dealers have escaped.

The ground troops take on another mission that day. After hiking three miles (4.8 km) through sweltering jungle, they reach a forty foot-long (12.2 m) pit filled with coca leaves and flammable chemicals (the first step in making cocaine). After gathering the clandestine lab's chemicals, shipping lists, and notes, they torch the pit. By midnight the men return to camp to rest before starting day sixty-seven of Ghost Zone.

Much of the world's cocaine comes from Central and South America. Mexico plays a key role in the global drug scene. In the west coast state of Sinaloa, narcotics reign supreme. As much as 70 percent of the cocaine supply imported to the U.S. from South America flows through Mexico—and much of it by way of Sinaloa.[2] Violence, too, is unrestrained.

In the city of Culiacán, Sinaloa, where fewer than a million people live, seven thousand murders occur each year—most drug related.[3] In 1995, Mexico's president, Ernesto Zedillo, called the drug trade "the most serious threat to national security that Mexico faces."[4] So many politicians participate in the drug trade that Mexico has been called a "narco-democracy."[5]

But Mexico is not the only drug mecca in the world. In Colombia, two of the most powerful drug organizations in the world have roots, in the cities of Medellín and Cali. Afghanistan, Myanmar, Morocco, and Nigeria contribute most of the world's supply of heroin. With the collapse of the Soviet Union, several Eastern European nations show an alarming increase in drug trading. A 1996 sting broke up a fifteen-year-old international drug ring begun and operated by Nigerian women. They had smuggled heroin from Pakistan, Thailand, and other South-east Asian countries to Amsterdam, Paris, Central America, Mexico, and cities throughout the United States.[6]

Illegal drug trafficking is truly a global affair—and an international beast of crime, greed, and corruption. With so many nations producing and transporting illegal drugs, the battleground cannot be confined to U.S. territory. Wherever drugs are cultivated, processed, and shipped, and their profits laundered, is battle turf. Given the international scope of the drug war, how would a change in the drug laws affect foreign relations? Would changes improve foreign relations? Or would they breach international treaties and weaken our resolve to end drug use?

Cooperation among Nations

The 1912 Hague Convention aimed to "suppress the nonmedical use of drugs."[7] Later, a number of other treaties were signed. In 1961, those treaties were consolidated into the Single Convention on Narcotic Drugs, which was ultimately signed by more than a hundred nations. The primary purpose of this treaty is to limit worldwide production of drugs to the amounts needed for scientific, medical, and industrial use.

In 1971, the Psychotropic Convention established international control of amphetamines, barbiturates, and hallucinogens. In 1988, forty-three nations signed the Vienna Convention to combat drug trafficking and money laundering. In addition to these treaties, the United States has worked out many agreements and treaties with individual nations.

A nation's laws take precedence over international law, so the United States could decriminalize and legalize certain drugs. It is often argued, however, that the treaties obligate us to maintain our current policy on heroin, marijuana, cocaine, and other drugs. Legal experts respond by pointing to Article 46 of the United Nations Single Convention on Narcotic Drugs, which states that any nation that has signed the treaty can release itself from it with six months' notice.[8]

Many governments, particularly those in nations struggling with poverty or shaky politics, refuse to cooperate with international drug control efforts. Iran, for example, is a major producer of opium and heroin. Since the 1979 revolution that established the Islamic Republic of Iran, U.S. diplomatic relations with Iran have been severed. This leaves the United States with no influence on Iranian drug trafficking except through interdiction (prohibition).

Some nations officially agree to cooperate, but widespread corruption among their officials and law enforcement agencies renders them ineffective. In 1994, Mexico's attorney general ordered federal police commanders to arrest important traffickers in their regions or face charges of complicity. Nonetheless, only minor figures were arrested and small amounts of cocaine seized and marijuana eradicated. According to Peter H. Smith, a political scientist at the University of California, the Mexican perception is "This is as much as we can do and it's more than what many countries do."[9]

Extradition

An important convention in international criminal justice is extradition—the surrender of an alleged criminal from one jurisdiction or country to another for prosecution. Extradition ensures that illegal drug producers and traffickers (or other criminals) can be brought to justice—no matter where they live or where they flee. At present, the United States has extradition treaties with over a hundred countries.[10] However, failures to extradite are common.

With our life-with-no-parole sentencing and death penalties for drug kingpins who are involved in murder, as most are, drug dealers try to avoid extradition at all costs. When the Colombian government extradited sixteen people, including the leader of the Medellín cartel, the cartel retaliated by murdering half the members of the Colombian Supreme Court and over a hundred court employees. Threatened with extradition a few years later, the drug dealers delivered a bouquet of flowers to a Colombian judge with a note saying that for every drug dealer extradited, they would murder ten judges. In 1995, six high-level members of the Cali cartel were arrested in Colombia. None were extradited to the United States.

Since 1984, we have had an extradition treaty with Pakistan, a major supplier of heroin and hashish. But the Pakistani government has repeatedly failed to extradite drug dealers to the United States. Other nations with whom we have extradition treaties are so corrupt that their courts either free the dealers or give them extremely lenient sentences.

Foreign Aid

Each year the U.S. president must decide whether or not a foreign nation is making an adequate effort to stop the production and transit of illicit drugs into the United States. If not, then the president can reduce or deny foreign aid and international loans. In 1996, President Clinton decertified (declared ineligible for aid in that year) six nations: Afghanistan, Myanmar, Iran, Nigeria, Syria, and Colombia. He again decertified Colombia in 1997.

The government doesn't always exercise this power to deny aid, especially if other interests are compelling. Even after Mexico's top drug-control officer was arrested on drug charges in 1997, Mexico retained its special trade agreements with the U.S. The policy can also backfire. When foreign aid to the Caribbean Community (fourteen small island nations) was decreased, fear rose that farmers would turn to illegal crops, such as marijuana.

To qualify for foreign aid, many poor nations are compelled to spend a disproportionate amount of their budget on the drug war. If we changed our drug policy, they could divert that money to social welfare programs to help their population with food, housing, medical care, education, and other crucial programs. And many governments are too poor to fight the drug war, even when they want to. Police in Osh, a small city in Russia, for instance, face a rapidly growing drug trade.[11] But the twenty-nine-member police force has only three Russian-made jeeps, a few guns, and a single walkie-talkie. Furthermore, with monthly salaries equal to only forty-five dollars, the members of the force are vulnerable to bribes and direct involvement in drug dealing.

A Foreign Affair

Following World War II, the United States opened its first foreign office of the DEA in Rome, Italy. Today, the DEA has hundreds of agents stationed throughout the world.

The State Department also plays a role in international drug control, with narcotics assistance units in major drug source and transit countries. To enforce international drug laws, U.S. agents train local people to fight the drug war. They also pay informants—often handsomely. In Colombia, informants received $1.5 million for information that led to the capture of several Cali cartel kingpins.

Another U.S. government agency with an important part in drug control is the Agency for International Development (AID). One of AID's main tasks is to help farmers find alternatives to illegal crops.

Many foreign governments welcome the presence of U.S. narcotics agents. However, asking these nations to get tough about drugs angers some of their citizens, who fear a hidden motive. As Gabriel García Márquez, one of Latin America's most eloquent spokespersons, sardonically observes, "The drug problem has been presented in reverse. In the U.S., addicts supply themselves as easily as they buy milk or newspapers. And yet we [Latin Americans] are accused of not doing enough against drug trafficking." Adds Marquez, "My worry is that the U.S. will use the fight against drug trafficking as a pretext for intervention."[12]

In 1995, two government officers from Thailand were denied U.S. visas because of suspected links to drug trafficking. An indignant spokesperson for Thailand warned the United States that it breached diplomatic ethics by interfering in Thai internal affairs.[13]

Much of our narcotics work consists of intelligence gathering. Explaining her resentment of the presence of U.S. narcotics agents in her country, one Latin American critic asked: "How would U.S. citizens feel about the KGB knocking on their doors, asking them questions or searching their homes?"

Another cause of resentment is the double standard DEA agents occasionally employ, as they act in other countries in ways that may be prohibited here. In Mexico, DEA agents secretly arrested a drug smuggler and transported him to a U.S. prison. While he awaited trial, DEA agents, together with Mexican police, searched his two homes without a legal search warrant. In the U.S. Supreme Court appeal of the case, the Justice Department argued that the Fourth Amendment's protection from unwarranted searches does not extend to foreigners, even in their own country. Justice William Brennan disagreed. "By respecting the rights of foreign nationals," he argued, "we encourage other nations to respect the rights of our citizens." And he added, "If we seek respect for law and order, we must observe these principles ourselves. Lawlessness breeds lawlessness."[14]

An essential part of U.S. control of foreign narcotics is the effort to help governments eradicate (destroy) illegal crops—the slow task of manually digging up the plants, or aerially spraying them.

Aerial eradication poses the risk that toxic chemicals can drift to other areas and contaminate people's eyes, skin, clothing, water, and food. Some herbicides may increase the risk of cancer and birth defects; others can damage the ecological system. If marijuana were legal, there would be no reason to damage the environment with potentially dangerous chemicals.

On the other hand, growers of illegal crops do their share of damage. In Peru, they have destroyed over half a million acres of tropical rain forest.[15] A change in our drug policy could increase the demand for drug products, which in turn could cause more land to be put under cultivation and cause farmers to further destroy the rain forests.

A Conflict of Interest

Some experts believe that a change in our drug laws would allow us to maintain a sounder foreign policy. In 1986, for example, the State Department supported a rebel group, the contras, in an attempt to overthrow Nicaragua's Sandinista government. This support included a payment of nearly $1 million to four companies distributing humanitarian aid—despite the fact that the companies were owned and operated by narcotics traffickers.

Our government also closed its eyes when we formed an alliance with General Manuel Antonio Noriega of Panama. For a time, General Noriega slyly befriended the DEA and the State Department, while taking $200 to $300 million in bribes from drug traffickers he promised to protect. The State Department had received reports on Noriega's illegal drug activities, but because of other interests, did nothing about Noriega's drug dealings until the *New York Times* ran an exposé. Only then did the U.S. State Department arrest him on drug charges.

If drugs were legalized in the U.S., drugs might no longer be a foreign affair (unless foreign nations with strict drug laws tried to stop us from providing drugs to them). Or, we could redirect our foreign drug policy toward helping those countries provide treatment and prevention programs for their citizens, perhaps through the United Nations.

Effect on Foreign Economies

In the free marketplace, if there is a demand for any product, people will be willing to supply it—legal or not. In poor regions, illegal drugs provide a way to earn a living and, occasionally, the chance to rise above poverty. In Kyrgyskln, Afghanistan, a ten-year-old boy can earn about thirty-five dollars for a few hours' work guiding a horse or mule laden with drugs through a mountain pass—the same amount his father will earn for a month of legitimate work. Throughout the world, hundreds of thousands of peasants earn far more money growing poppy, coca, and marijuana than they could earn from legal crops. In Bolivia, where over three hundred thousand people grow coca, workers can earn thirty dollars a day, which is three times what they could earn harvesting yucca or corn.[16] Eradicating drug crops angers the peasants and can cause political unrest. "We know the people hate us," said the leader of a drug raid in Bolivia. "When we do this, we're taking their livelihood away."[17]

Groups in a number of countries have organized protests against the national drug policy. The scene here is in South Africa.

If drugs were legal and the demand for them increased, these people could continue growing their crops and would not need to ally with drug dealers. On the other hand, legalization would reduce the price of drugs and force them once again into poverty. Just as banana, corn, and other legal crops often do not support peasant families, cannabis, coca, or heroin crops—unless they remained illegal in other nations—may not provide adequate incomes.

A change in the U.S. drug laws affects foreign economies in other ways. In 1992, for example, the central bank of Peru received up to $5 million a day through drug sales and money laundering. The loss of this income could have plunged Peru into an economic crisis. And if the economy in one Latin American country collapses, other Latin American nations may be affected. A collapse also would mean that huge debt repayments to American banks would end, which could jeopardize some U.S. banks.[18]

A Losing Battle

Trying to control international narcotics supplies is like riding a seesaw. When one country "pushes down" its supply, there is always another to "pop up" and take its place. Early in the 1960s, Turkey grew most of the opium for the heroin smuggled into the United States. (The opium was grown in Turkey but processed in France.) This "French Connection" was busted in 1973, and the Turkish government cooperated with the United States and France to eradicate most of Turkey's illicit opium crop.

When the Turkish supply was pushed down, a new supply popped up in Mexico. The United States pressured Mexico, and Mexican heroin imports went from nearly 90 percent of the U.S. supply to a third of it, another push down for foreign narcotics control. The new pop up? First, the Golden Triangle of Burma, Thailand, and Laos; and later, the Golden Crescent of Afghanistan, Pakistan, and Iran.

Enforcement clearly affects the supply side of the picture. It also affects the quality. Mark Kleinman of Harvard's Kennedy School of Government conducted a study of the illegal marijuana market. He found that when tighter border controls reduced marijuana imports, the slack was taken up by American growers. Within a decade, American growers were producing at least a third of the marijuana sold in the United States.

Change around the World

Despite the international treaties and the firm stand against drugs that persists in the United States, several countries have recently moved toward drug law reform. Following the more liberal course set by the Netherlands, Germany's highest court ruled in 1992 that outlawing the personal use and possession of marijuana and hashish is unconstitutional. Although many conservative German politicians criticized the ruling, a surprising number of elected officials and German newspapers and magazines welcomed it. "I would look positively on any policy that decriminalizes the use of soft drugs," stated Germany's interior minister, Friedel Lapple, in a radio interview.[19]

In 1994, the high court of Colombia, a country rife with drug dealing and trafficking, legalized the personal use and possession of marijuana, hashish, cocaine, and hallucinogens. Colombia's justices argued that Colombian citizens have a constitutional right to the personal use of these drugs.[20]

Most other nations do not show signs of liberalizing their drug policies. Singapore routinely executes those who defy its strict drug laws—even for possession of a small amount. In 1994, a Dutch engineer was caught by customs officials with nearly ten pounds of heroin hidden in his suitcase. His family received this telegram: *Death sentence passed. . . .Will be carried into effect on 23.9.94. Visit him on 20.9.94. Claim body on 23.9.94.* Signed: Superintendent, Changi Prison, Singapore.[21]

China, too, shows little tolerance for drug traffickers. In a public sentencing attended by thousands of people, thirty-five Chinese drug dealers were paraded in front of the crowd, then shot.[22] Only a few Chi-

Along with Singapore and China, Malaysia takes a hard line against drug trafficking.

nese citizens use heroin, but the number is increasing. With their display of severe punishment, Chinese officials hope to dissuade citizens from using heroin or other illegal drugs.

As long as nations refuse or are too politically corrupt to cooperate in the drug war, the international drug trade will never end. We have already waged two wars against drugs. To wage a real war with troops, guns, tanks, and bombs is unimaginable. Given the hilly terrain where drugs are grown, as well as the cunning savagery of drug traffickers, the outcome of a war against the dozens of nations that supply drugs or provide shelter for money laundering would dwarf our failure in Vietnam. And the push down–pop up cycle shows that any victory would be short lived.

To legalize drugs altogether would put the issue on a different footing—from eradication and law enforcement to economic competition and economic survival. If drugs remain somewhat profitable, farmers will grow them in place of food products. However, many farmers cannot survive growing food crops, and growing legal drug crops will probably also fail to lift them out of poverty. All in all, it's not a pretty picture, regardless of what occurs.

CHAPTER 12

Changing the System

Members of Our Church, a religious organization in Cane Hill, Arkansas, believed that the Religious Freedom Restoration Act of 1993 entitled them to grow and use marijuana as a religious sacrament. They also provided free marijuana to people who used it for medical reasons.

After informing the county sheriff of their plans to grow and distribute marijuana on May 1, 1994, eleven members of the church planted ninety marijuana seedlings on the church grounds. This was done in view of local television and newspaper reporters. Some months later, members of the church, who claim a code of behavior that is "moral in nature and relating to our worship with God, and that marijuana is part of that," planted several hundred more seedlings.

In the spirit of nineteenth-century philosopher Henry David Thoreau, these people were defying a law (against growing marijuana) that they considered unjust. Their intention was to change that law. "The function of someone who is committing an act of civil disobedience," explained founding church member Reverend Tom

At pot protests and weed-ins, demonstrators call for legalized marijuana.

Brown, "is to confront something they see as evil. And marijuana prohibition is evil."[1]

Brown was later arrested and convicted as an "alleged drug kingpin" for giving away over fifteen pounds (6.8 kg) of marijuana. He received a ten-year prison sentence, was fined $17,500, and his farm was forfeited to the state.

Each year, throughout the nation, protesters, many bearing a striking resemblance to the hippies of the 1960s, gather for "weed-ins" and pot protests. The 1995 HempFest, a rock concert to support legalizing marijuana, attracted more than fifty thousand participants to Seattle, Washington. One annual protest—the Atlanta Pot Festival—in some years draws twenty-five thousand supporters. Even though police make arrests for possession of marijuana, hundreds of people openly smoke joints. As one commented, "What are they [police] going to do. . . arrest 10,000 people?"[2]

In Vermont, drug reform activists organized the Vermont Coalition against Prohibition. In addition to a program of educating the public about the various uses of hemp, the group engages in nonviolent demonstrations. They once launched marijuana seeds from twin-engine rockets. On another occasion, they packed seeds onto "warheads" at a fairground. Group members vowed to plant hemp seeds across the entire state of Vermont, much the way Johnny Appleseed planted apple seeds long ago.[3]

Unlike these protesters, most people in search of drug law reform take a quieter road and adopt a more moderate agenda. Some merely want to make marijuana available for medical or industrial use. Others lobby the federal government to fund needle exchange programs for intravenous drug users or to make syringes legal to stem the spread of HIV and other communicable diseases. Still others work to make drug use and abuse a health, rather than a criminal, issue.

Who Is Calling for Change?

Who are the people calling for change? A bunch of Lollapalooza fans seeking to legalize pot? Discouraged prosecutors who believe that trying to bust major drug cartels and crime organizations is akin to fighting a tidal wave with a sandbag wall? Environmentalists who worry about attacking marijuana and opium plants with chemicals that can seriously damage the ecosystem? Disenchanted law enforcement officials whose experience demonstrates that laws can't stop drug abuse and who understand the temptations that corrupt their colleagues? Neighbors weary of seeing ruthless drug dealers take over their streets? Those who think that what they do with their bodies is no one else's business? People suffering with glaucoma, cancer, or other illnesses who use marijuana for pain relief or to treat their conditions?

They Are All of These.

Those who propose repealing the drug laws are found everywhere. Some are conservative political thinkers such as economist Milton Friedman, former secretary of state George P. Schultz, conservative Republican, Richard Cowman, and William F. Buckley Jr., editor of *National Review*. In 1995, even Speaker of the House Newt Gingrich remarked, "Either legalize it or get rid of it."[4]

Not surprisingly, drug law reformers can also be found among liberal citizens. The late Timothy Leary, who conducted research on hallucinogenic drugs at Harvard during the 1960s, made this admission in a speech in 1994: "I make it a point to take every illegal drug at least once a year."[5] And hippie Stephen Gaskin, who led a bus caravan from San Francisco to rural Tennessee in 1971 to start a commune, in 1995 vowed to make legalizing marijuana a top priority on his agenda.[6]

A few advocates of change can be found among law enforcement officers, politicians, and judges. For almost a decade, Kurt L. Schmoke, mayor of Baltimore, Maryland, proposed legalizing drugs.[7] A former prosecutor, Schmoke, whose city is one of the most drug ridden in the nation, is convinced that legalization is the only answer. House Democrats Nancy Pelosi, Henry Waxman, and Barney Frank all support the distribution of marijuana for medical purposes.[8]

Whenever these people speak out for legalization, however, they risk public disapproval and, in some cases, damage to their careers. Joycelyn Elders, surgeon general during the first Clinton administration, was asked about legalizing drugs at a luncheon for reporters. When she said it could reduce the crime rate and offered to study the issue further, she was roundly criticized.

Those calling for a saner drug policy include many conservative people, such as former secretary of state George Schultz.

Some politicians refuse to even discuss the issue. During the 1996 election, the Washington Citizens for Hemp Reform polled all the candidates in the state's forty-nine legislative districts to determine their position on the decriminalization of marijuana for medical, industrial, and personal use. Out of the 201 candidates polled, a mere 20 responded to the questionnaire.[9]

In addition to individuals, numerous groups and organizations are working for a change in our drug laws. I-CARE is an organization of nurses working to make marijuana legal for medical patients. The National Organization for the Reform of Marijuana Law (NORML) works to educate both the public and policymakers about marijuana and marijuana laws. In 1992, Richard Cowman, a former president of the Republican Club of Yale University, was appointed director of NORML. Under his leadership, the number of NORML chapters throughout the United States has grown to over a hundred. Since its founding in 1970, NORML has filed many lawsuits, one of which led to the development of Marinol (the synthetic marijuana pill). Drug reform is on the agenda of several think tanks (organizations that employ scholars to research issues and report their findings), including the Cato Institute, the Rand Corporation, and Lindesmith Center, which was funded by George Soros, a successful businessman. Besides publishing academic papers, researchers at some of these think tanks hold seminars to educate people about an issue and to foster debate on the subject. For example, Ethan Nadelmann of the Lindesmith Center regularly brings together journalists, lawyers, academics, drug treatment program administrators, and even drugs users and addicts to discuss drug laws.

The Drug Policy Foundation is a Washington, D.C., think tank devoted to the issue of drug law reform. One of the foundation's major tasks is to inform members of Congress about the issue. Staff members hold forums for legislators and policymakers, and the foundation sponsors an annual conference at which experts from around the world convene to share research and ideas.

Despite the increasing membership and support these various groups are gaining, changing the drug laws remains an uphill battle, largely because many Americans are so opposed to drug use and so fearful of drugs like marijuana, Ecstasy, LSD, and, especially, cocaine and heroin.

Since 1973, the National Opinion Research Center (NORC) has polled a sample of Americans about the issue of legalizing marijuana. In 1978, nearly one-third of the adults and over the half of high school seniors and first-year college students surveyed believed that marijuana should be legalized. During the 1980s' crack epidemic, pollsters found far less support—fewer than one in five respondents believed that marijuana should be legalized.[10]

In telephone surveys conducted in Nebraska and Pennsylvania in 1994, nearly nine out of ten people (89 percent) believed that marijuana should be legal for medical use.[11] The victories of referendums to legalize medical marijuana in California and Arizona in 1996 showed that a majority of voters in those states support that position.

Decriminalizing or legalizing marijuana for nonmedical use attracts far less public support, while legalizing hard drugs such as heroin is even less popular. In fact, when polled, the majority of Americans, including many young people, strongly oppose the idea of legalizing all drugs.

Much of this opposition is grounded in the fear that if drugs were legal, their use would increase. In a 1995 Gallup poll of adults, most repondents agreed that legalization of marijuana would send the message that "drugs are okay to use"—a message few people, even drug reform advocates, want to give. Other surveys validate this fear. In one survey, 10 percent said that if marijuana were legalized, they would be tempted to try it. If drugs other than marijuana were legalized, some of those already using marijuana claim they would be open to experimenting with drugs they currently avoid; 2 percent of those who had never used cocaine said they would try it.[12]

A further fear is that increased drug use will exacerbate myriad problems already associated with drugs—apathy in school, burnout, drug-related crime, HIV-infected and drug-addicted newborns, industrial and motor accidents, overdoses, and deaths.

Bringing about a Change

There are a number of ways to work to change drug laws and drug enforcement policy. These include:

Civil disobedience. Acts of civil disobedience like smoke-ins, in which protesters smoke marijuana in public and in view of police to defy the laws, force the issue into the courts if participants are arrested. When their cases are tried, they have the opportunity to present arguments for changing or striking down the law.

The strength of civil disobedience is that a small number of people—the defendants and the judge or justices—can bring about sweeping social change. Civil disobedience has several drawbacks, however. First, the judge may refuse to allow testimony about the injustice of the law. Instead, the defense may be confined to the particular charge. Second, the sentence may be severe. Going to jail to defend a civil liberty may be noble, but spending years in prison when there are other effective ways to achieve the same goal runs the risk of martyrdom, that is, unreasonable sacrifice for a cause. As one lawyer who defended the minister from Our Church suggested, the law could have been tested by planting a few plants instead of several hundred. That way, he could have stayed out of jail and continued his efforts.

Civil disobedience may alienate mainstream voters and conservative policymakers whose support may be needed. It can also erode our legal system. After all, if every group—with individual, and perhaps self-serving, agendas—resorted to civil disobedience, the result would be chaos. Taken to an extreme, civil disobedience can cause lawlessness, a situation that is usually more dangerous than the problem the groups are protesting.

Day in court. Many people—millions in fact—break drug laws. Their intention is not to be arrested. Still, once arrested, they may find themselves in court trying to change the law so that they will be acquitted. In states which have approved medical marijuana, those arrested for using or prescribing marijuana can try to use the state law as their defense in court.

Others seek change through class-action lawsuits (suits that involve an entire group of people instead of one individual) and other lawsuits. For example, some people oppose random drug testing. When an Oregon seventh grader refused to submit to a drug test required of his school's football players, he was denied a place on the team. In response, his family challenged the legality of random drug testing in a suit against the local school board. In 1995, the case reached the U.S. Supreme Court and the Court upheld the local school board's right to subject student athletes to random drug testing. Had they decided against the drug tests, however, the decision would have paved the way to stop other random drug testing.

A protestor at a smoke-in

Many important changes in American society have arisen from judicial decisions. These include the decision to make abortion a legal choice *(Roe v. Wade)* and the decision to desegregate public schools *(Brown v. Board of Education)*. Yet as the suit against random drug testing of school athletes proves, there is a caveat here: Just as the courts can repeal the drug laws, they can also make them stricter.

The public forum. Another path toward reform of drug laws is through public debate and voter referendums. Small New England towns retain a truly democratic form of government. Instead of having representatives or a council make local laws, each citizen votes on the measure at a town meeting. In Starks, Maine, in 1992, the Maine Vocals, an organization working for the legalization of pot, asked its members to attend the town meeting. A third of the voting population of the tiny village turned out for the meeting. Many were there to support the Maine Vocals, who had mustered their forces for the meeting. Thus, when a member of the Maine Vocals moved to put drug reform on the agenda and called for a vote, their large turnout gave them an advantage. By a narrow margin of three votes, the resolution to change the drug law passed.[13]

Drug law reformers in several states, including California, Colorado, Arizona, and Oregon, have tried to put the issue on the ballot. After California governor Pete Wilson vetoed the state bill to make marijuana available as a legal prescription, reformers placed Compassionate Use Act 215 on the ballot in 1996 to allow California voters to make the decision instead of legislators. The result was the approval of the medical use of marijuana.

Voter referendums take enormous effort. Thousands of signatures must be collected to put the measure on a ballot. This requires paid staff members, office supplies, and other costs that can run into millions of dollars. But voter referendums can also overturn a court decision. In 1975, the Alaska Supreme Court ruled that citizens have a constitutional right to possess up to four ounces of marijuana for personal use. "Big Brother cannot, in the name of public health," said Justice Jay Rabinowitz in his opinion in the landmark case, *Ravin v. State of Alaska*, "dictate to anyone what he can eat or drink or smoke in the privacy of his own home."[14] Fifteen years later, though, in 1991, Alaska's voters recriminalized marijuana and made possession of it punishable by ninety days in jail and a one-thousand-dollar fine.

In the arm of government. If reform does occur, many people believe that it will happen where drug laws were enacted in the first place—the legislature. Since legislators have the power to enact laws, they also have the power to repeal or change them.

By 1997, thirty-six state legislatures had enacted laws to make marijuana legal for medical use and bills were pending in several other states.

Support from politicians, especially those on the national level, is limited. Those who take a stand risk defeat in their next election. After all, most public servants work to reflect the voices of their constituents—the people who voted them into office. As Ron Kampia, director of the Marijuana Policy Project, observes, "Politicians follow what they perceive to be the will of their constituents, and their constituents do not want marijuana legalized."[15] In a National Opinion Research Center survey, only one out of five people sampled said they thought marijuana should be made legal. Kampia suggests that organizations wishing to shift this sentiment should work to change the voters' opinions, rather than lobby the legislators.

When the Constitution was framed, our founders built change into our system of government. This is essential. Substantial change, however, often comes slowly, and sometimes at a significant social cost. For example, during the Civil War and World War I, before passage of the Conscientious Objection Act allowed exemption of pacifists from serving in the military, hundreds of pacifists and war resisters were imprisoned; a few were even executed.

In a 1996 Gallup poll, 85 percent of respondents opposed legalization of drugs. Having smoked marijuana in the past no longer bars a candidate from office, as Susan Molinari, a recently elected congressional representative learned. Admitting to a current drug habit, on the other hand, can bring a career to an abrupt end. Despite the candor of a few public officials, most politicians echo the general public view and resist the idea of ending drug prohibition. Ironically, many liberal politicians use drug laws as a chance to show their conservative constituents how "tough" they can be on crime.

As long as public opinion remains staunchly on the side of drug laws, even officials who privately call for change hesitate to take that position publicly. This is especially true for police officers and prosecutors, whose job it is to uphold, not criticize, the law, and for politicians, whose jobs depend on public approval.

The courts also remain unlikely sites for legalization. Judges continue to uphold the legality of forfeiture laws and drug testing and to broaden the definition of search and seizure. Moreover, the Supreme Court justices have refused to hear numerous drug cases; when they do take on a case, they tend to uphold and not liberalize drug laws.

With such overwhelming support of drug prohibition, total repeal of the drug laws is unlikely to occur. Groups such as NORML, the Sentencing Project, Families against Mandatory Minimums, and others working for reform are relatively small and focus their energy on limited goals, such as legalizing marijuana for medical use or reducing penalties for first-time, nonviolent drug offenses. Still, as anthropologist Margaret Mead once said, "Never doubt that a small group of thoughtful committed citizens can change the world: Indeed, it is the only thing that ever has."

CHAPTER 13

What's the Gamble?

On August 9, 1995, fifty-three-year-old guitarist and singer Jerry Garcia of the Grateful Dead died of a heart attack at a drug rehabilitation center. During his life, Garcia used an array of drugs—LSD, tobacco, heroin, marijuana. They may well have hastened his death.

Many other people have chosen to use illicit drugs for a variety of reasons. Some people believe drugs help them express their creativity, find clarity, and enhance their senses. Some drugs help people stay awake. For some people, drugs seem to offer an escape, albeit temporary, from the physical or mental pain of their lives.[1] As they did for Garcia, though, drugs usually represent both good and evil—or at least pleasure and pain.

Drug laws affect many areas of life, from crime and justice to economics, foreign policy, and ecology. That is why changing or repealing the laws is so complicated—and why the success or failure of a change is difficult to predict. Nor is changing the drug laws and drug policy a magic elixir. Many individual and societal problems will remain

Jerry Garcia in concert

and, in fact, changing the drug laws may create new ones. Indeed, the outcome is a gamble.

The Legal Twist

For over eighty years, we have had laws against drugs. We keep adding more laws and tougher laws. Yet millions of Americans persist in using illicit drugs. During the early 1960s, one out of every fifty Americans had tried an illicit drug.[2] Now, one out of every three has. We can only wonder how many more might have tried illicit drugs if they had been legal.

After passage of the Volstead Act prohibiting the manufacture and sale of alcohol, far fewer Americans drank. Death from cirrhosis of the liver (a disease often caused by drinking) fell to a third of the former rate. Arrests for public drunkenness and disorderly conduct dropped to half the former rate. And admissions to state mental hospitals for alcoholic psychosis declined by more than half.[3] When the Volstead Act was repealed, alcohol was again legal, and many more Americans drank. In a short while, the number of adults consuming alcoholic beverages doubled.

As the law kept many people from drinking, so current drug laws keep some people from using illicit drugs. The question is: How many people? Most people wish to be law-abiding citizens. Some respect laws too much to break them, even if they don't always agree that a law is just. Others won't risk the consequences of violating a law. The shame of being arrested, the fear of going to jail, even the expense of hiring a defense lawyer keeps many people from smoking pot or using other illicit drugs. Still others, primarily adults, avoid using an illicit drug because they don't know where or how to obtain it, or they are reluctant to go where drugs are sold or meet drug dealers. Some experts, perhaps out on a limb, argue that legalizing drugs would give society a chance to mature in its reaction to dangerous drugs. While more people might use drugs, fewer people would abuse them.

David Musto, a historian of drug policy, suggests that public attitudes go through regular cycles. First, a small group of people experiment with a new drug. They promote it. The drug's popularity grows. Then the public learns about its dangers. As a result, the drug is prohibited, while the public grows intolerant of those who abuse it. Then the drug's negative image spreads to the poor. Finally, use declines.

Other experts agree that drug use is cyclical and argue that drug use will decrease regardless of the laws. Arnold Trebach, founder of the Drug Policy Foundation, points out that with the exception of fourteen years of Prohibition, alcohol has always been part of American society—and legal. In 1830, Americans consumed more liquor than ever before or after—more than seven gallons absolute proof per person.[4] By the end of the 1800s, annual consumption dropped to less than two gallons per person. "These changes," noted Trebach, "took place within an atmosphere of legality."

Theories such as Trebach's, however, ignore the rise in drinking when Prohibition was repealed. They also overlook the widespread alcoholism, compulsive gambling, and cigarette addiction that exist now, despite their legality and the restrictions placed on their use.

Also, a substance legal for adults but restricted for minors becomes attractive to young people searching for ways to defy their elders, act grown-up, or test the waters. More than 90 percent of all high school seniors have tried alcohol; more than two-thirds have tried cigarettes.[5]

Buyer Beware

Buying drugs on the street keeps users ignorant of a drug's true potency, which can lead them to overdose, a particularly serious problem among heroin users. Furthermore, to stretch their profits, some dealers "cut" hard drugs with substances like arsenic and strychnine, which can cause severe complications, including death.

Since repeal of the Volstead Act, the government has had strict labeling laws so consumers know the exact percentage of alcohol in their drinks. If drugs were legal and subject to the same government quality control, drug users could be better-informed consumers.

A Saner Policy

Government regulation of hard drugs allows addicts to get a legal supply of drugs. Government clinics provide addicts with medical supervision. Government regulation keeps drugs affordable and thus removes the pressure to commit crime. This model, called "harm reduction," is based on the premise that a drug-free society is an unrealistic goal.[6]

In 1994, Switzerland began a nationwide experiment to offer Swiss addicts the chance to go to a clinic where heroin, cocaine, and methadone would be administered by a health professional. The program has been highly successful. With careful supervision and a clean environment, few medical problems arose, and the health of addicts in the program improved. Nor did a black market for heroin develop. And the belief that addicts have an insatiable craving for heroin develop false. When offered unlimited amounts of heroin, addicts discovered that large dosages provided less of a "flash" than lower doses.[7] Based on its success, the Swiss government expanded the program, and the Dutch and German governments made plans to start similar programs.

Repeal of the 1981 Model Drug Paraphernalia Act, which bans the sale of water pipes, bongs, and other apparatus used to smoke marijuana and hashish, would offer health benefits to users. Because most of the carcinogens (cancer-causing substances) in hashish and marijuana are water soluble, the paraphernalia allows water to absorb the carcinogens in the smoke, which makes marijuana less harmful.

A change in drug policy could give IV drug users access to sterile needles, which could curb the tranmission of HIV and other diseases.

Most people did not buy the first drugs they used. Instead, they were "turned on" or given a drug by someone they knew. Many times these were people looking for new customers, who could help them support their own drug habit. The average heroin seller, for instance, relies on the support of three heavy users.[8] Legalization might take away an addict's incentive to recruit new users, and it would curtail the supplier's incentive to find a broader customer base. In fact, if drug prices fell, suppliers would probably advertise, as the tobacco and liquor industries have done for years. Instead of Joe Camel, we might see Heroin Harry, Cocaine Charlie, or Mary Jane Marijuana.

Many young people who smoke marijuana want to see it legalized. It would probably still be off-limits to them, as alcohol and cigarettes are supposed to be, and legalization would make it more difficult (but not impossible) for them to buy drugs. Stiffer government regulations for the sale of alcohol and cigarettes make it more difficult for minors to buy beer and cigarettes than to puchase marijuana, LSD, and other illicit drugs (though many teenagers appear to have no problem rising to that challenge). On the contrary, illicit drugs are easy to find *precisely because they are illegal and unregulated.*

The Big "What If"

Based on the addiction rates of drugs that are already legal, experts have made predictions about the increase in drug use—and addiction—that might occur with legalization.

Not all smokers and drinkers are addicted: some can quit at will. However, practically all regular smokers are addicted to nicotine. Even though smoking has declined in recent years, half of those who smoke report having tried to quit and failing.[9] The other half didn't even try.

Alcohol is less addictive than nicotine. Still, when they drink, many people, especially teenagers today, binge; others become alcoholic, sometimes shortly after beginning to drink. The estimated number of alcoholics in the U.S. is 10 to 18 million—quite a high percentage considering that no more than 100 million people drink.[10]

Researchers have found that most controlled drugs are less addictive than nicotine but more addictive than alcohol. In one laboratory experiment, rats were given unlimited access to cocaine. The rats preferred taking cocaine to eating or sleeping. They ingested increasingly large amounts until they died from overdosing.[11] While it is impossible to draw exact parallels to humans, according to Jack Henningfield of the Baltimore Addiction Research Center, one in six users will be unable to quit on their own. Other experts place addiction rates twice as high, at one in three. Using these various rates of addiction, if drugs, especially cocaine and heroin, were legalized, some experts predict that the number of addicts could increase from the about 3 million we currently have to 20 million.[12] Other experts place the "at risk" population at 12 percent of the total U.S. population, or about 29 million people.[13] And a few suggest that as many as 50 million people could become addicted to drugs if all laws against them were repealed. To put that in some perspective, we already have 51 million smokers, and most are addicted to nicotine.

We already have a shortage of treatment programs. If drugs were legalized, would not the need for centers increase substantially? How will we raise funds to pay for treatment if drug abuse rises? Will everyone who needs treatment agree to it and will they find it available?

Even if all serious drug users underwent treatment and rehabilitation, it would still leave us with addicts. Why? Chemical dependence has no permanent cure; the battle against it is lifelong. Relapse is always a possibility. Despite medical advances and new treatments, from methadone to acupuncture, no treatment is 100 percent successful. And not all drug abusers are ready or willing to undergo treatment.

Most observers agree that any illicit drug use has the potential to cause harm. But despite the serious problems habitual users have and inflict on others, not all users are drug abusers or addicts. Why they aren't remains, in large part, a mystery. This is one of the most compelling reasons for drug control. In fact, it is one of the most worrisome risks of legalization—that there would be more problems caused by more drug overdoses and more addiction.

In contrast to the predictions of soaring rates of abuse, a survey conducted by the Drug Policy Foundation asked respondents whether they would try drugs if they became legal. Only 10 percent of those who had never smoked marijuana said they would be tempted to try it. Even fewer people who had never tried cocaine—2 percent—said they would be tempted to try it. This suggests that the number of people who would start using drugs is far less than predicted.

During the past decade, Americans have become more health conscious. This has contributed to a decline in both smoking and drinking among adults. Conceivably, more effective prevention programs than we currently have could keep more Americans from using drugs, even if they were legalized.

The call for change is not just about legalizing drugs—be it one drug, some drugs, or all drugs. Even without legalization, we can change our drug policy and the way we enforce it. As Mayor Kurt Schmoke of Baltimore, an advocate of legalizing drugs, suggests, "The fight on drugs should be led by the surgeon general, and not the attorney general."[14]

Without total repeal of all the drug laws, we can change the way we regulate drugs, allowing doctors to prescribe marijuana for medical treatment, heroin for addicts, and narcotics for those who suffer from chronic, uncontrollable pain.

Without an end to prohibition, we can reduce the Draconian sentences we now impose on nonviolent drug offenders who neither need such harsh sentences to rehabilitate themselves nor deserve it for the crimes they have committed. This would ease the strain on our criminal justice system and free it to focus on violent crimes.

We can allow cannabis low in THC to be grown and used for fuel, fiber, and industrial products.

We started this book with a look at a cannabis cafe in Amsterdam. Perhaps we can end it with another Dutch scene—the annual Cannabis Cup held in Amsterdam during the third weekend of November, generally coinciding with Thanksgiving weekend.

Each year, while Americans are feasting on turkey, sweet potatoes, and pumpkin pie, a few hundred Americans fly to Amsterdam instead to get stoned out of their minds at the annual Cannabis Cup, sponsored

A display of the Cannabis Cup winner in Holland

by *High Times*, the bimonthly newspaper that promotes marijuana cultivation and use. Large rewards go to the Cup winner—the grower of the best marijuana—who will be able to sell the plant's seeds for as much as thirty dollars a seed.

For some, the idea of a weekend of being stoned, partying with hundreds of other potheads, dope dealers, hippies, and adventurers from all over the world is, well, heaven on earth.

Legalization could provide an experience resembling that of the passengers on the *Titantic*, the famed ocean liner whose passengers thought they had embarked on a luxury voyage—until the ship sank, carrying hundreds to their deaths in the turbulent sea. Legalizing marijuana or any other drug may not be as risky an adventure as the 1912 voyage of the *Titantic*. Nor is it likely to result in events as radical as the Cannabis Cup. But for the United States, with our urban problems, our many troubled families, and our other challenges, it clearly would be a journey through uncharted waters.

It is easy to look at the Dutch model and hope that their drug policy can work for us. But we lack their strict gun control and their compassion for addicts, their inclusion of them as "part of the Dutch family."[15] As a result of these cultural differences, the Dutch program is not a safe predictor of what would occur here. Nor is the Dutch solution perfect. While they formerly had half as many youthful marijuana users as we did, marijuana use among Dutch youth is now rising sharply. And there are fears that the heavy competition among cafes will lead some to push harder drugs to stay profitable.

In short, we *just don't know what would happen if we legalize marijuana,* and we are even more at a loss about the risks of legalizing all drugs. All we can do is guess.

We can step up our fight against drugs or we can retreat from the battle altogether. Each side has some supporters who are reasonable and some who are fanatic.

Or, we can look for a middle road, and carefully change some of our laws and policies, resume the war on poverty, and search for healthful, hopeful ways of living.

Notes

Chapter 1

1. Jeff Kaye, "The Corner Hashish Joint," *Los Angeles Times* (Dec. 10, 1992); Michael Pollan, "How Pot Has Grown," *New York Times Magazine* (Feb. 19, 1995).
2. "Permissive Drug Policy Keeps Lid On," *Cleveland Plain Dealer* (Dec. 10, 1993).
3. "Marijuana Club Leader Arrested in San Francisco," *New York Times* (Oct. 12, 1996).
4. Quoted in Christopher S. Wren, "Votes on Marijuana Are Stirring Debate," *New York Times* (Nov. 17, 1996).
5. Executive Office, the White House, *The National Drug Control Strategy*; report (1996), 79.
6. This includes the federal expenditure and the $15 billion spent by state and local governments.
7. Stephen Gaskin, "Cannabis Spirituality," *High Times* (Dec. 1996), 48–52.
8. Malmoud A. ElSohly, *Quarterly Report: Potency Monitoring Project* (1994), cited in letter from Paul Armentano to Lee Brown (July 21, 1995).
9. National Household Survey on Drug Abuse, reported in "Fact Sheet: Drug Use Trends," Office of National Drug Control Policy (July 1996).
10. Garry Trudeau, "Getting over Getting Stoned," *Time* (Sept. 16, 1996), 94.

Chapter 2

1. "Genetic Study Leads to Marijuana Target on the Brain's Cells," *New York Times* (Aug. 9, 1990).
2. Philip J. Hilts, "How the Brain Is Stimulated by Marijuana Is Discovered," *New York Times* (July 21, 1990).
3. Hilts, "How the Brain Is Stimulated by Marijuana."
4. Helen E. Fisher, *Anatomy of Love* (New York: W. W. Norton, 1992), 51–58.
5. Ronald K. Siegel, *Intoxication* (New York: E. P. Dutton, 1989), 43–44.
6. "Rethinking Rites of Passage: Substance Abuse in America's Campuses." A Report by the Commission on Substance Abuse at Colleges and Universities, (June 1994).

7. Cited in Mathea Falco, *The Making of a Drug-Free America* (New York: Random House, 1994), 25.

8. David T. Courtwright, *Dark Paradise: Opiate Addiction in America before 1940* (Cambridge: Harvard University Press, 1982), 51.

9. Cited in Courtwright, *Dark Paradise*, 97.

10. David F. Musto, *The American Disease: Origins of Narcotic Control* (New York: Oxford University Press, 1987), 132.

11. Edward M. Brecher, ed., *Licit and Illicit Drugs* (Boston: Little, Brown, 1972).

12. *Webb et al. v. United States*, cited in Musto, *The American Disease*, 282.

13. "Crusade Brought Tempest," *Cleveland Plain Dealer* (Feb. 21, 1994).

14. Quoted in Paul Feldman and Leslie Berger, "Drug Czar Sells New Strategy to L.A. Audience," *Los Angeles Times* (Oct. 24, 1993).

Chapter 3

1. B. Drummon Ayres Jr., "2 Students Enter Pleas in Campus Drug Raid," *New York Times* (June 15, 1991).

2. Ibid.

3. These cases are from Eric Schlosser, "Marijuana and the Law," *Atlantic Monthly* (Sept. 1994), 89.

4. Ibid.

5. Vincent T. Bugliosi, *The Phoenix Solution* (Beverly Hills: Dove, 1996), 230.

6. Doug Dillaman, *Passport to Justice* (Washington D.C.: FAMM), 21.

7. Julie Stewart, "Letter," *FAMM-Gram Newsletter* (Oct. 1994/Jan. 1995).

Chapter 4

1. Vincent T. Bugliosi, *The Phoenix Solution: Getting Serious about Winning America's Drug War* (Beverly Hills: Dove, 1996), 248.

2. Joseph B. Treaster, "Huge Drug Tunnel from Mexico into U.S. Is Found," *New York Times* (June 3, 1993).

3. Joseph P. Fried, "Dog Arrives at Kennedy from Colombia Implanted with Five Pounds of Cocaine," *New York Times* (Dec. 6, 1994).

4. U.S. Dept. of Justice, *Drugs, Crime, and the Justice System: A National Report,* (December 1992), 44.

5. "DEA Herbicide under Fire from Hawaii Residents," online news report (Oct. 17, 1996).

6. Ed Vaughan, "National Guard Involvement in the Drug War," paper (Oct. 1994), reprinted by NORML.

7. Bugliosi, *The Phoenix Solution*, 80–81.

8. Bureau of Justice Statistics, reported in Fox Butterfield, "More in U.S. Are in Prisons, Report Says," *New York Times* (Aug. 10, 1995).

9. Ibid.

10. Nicholas D. Kristof, "Japanese Say No to Crime: Tough Methods at a Price," *New York Times* (May 14, 1995).

11. "Drugs and Crime across America: Police Chiefs Speak Out," report by Peter D. Hart Research Associates (1996), 4.

12. U.S. Department of Justice, "Drug-Related Crime," fact sheet, (Sept. 1994), 2.

13. Jan Hoffman, "Prosecutors Resist Shift to Drug Center for Felons," *New York Times* (Oct. 21, 1996).

14. Statistics from interview with Mark Mauer, Sentencing Project (Nov. 18, 1996).

15. William Bowman, "Don't Destroy the Family Unit," *Houston Chronicle* (June 23, 1995).

Chapter 5

1. Reported by Nat Hentoff, *Washington Post*, date unknown.

2. Robert E. Bauman, "Take It Away: License to Steal," *National Review* (Feb. 20, 1995), 36.

3. Tom Morganthau et al., "Uncivil Liberties?" *Newsweek* (Apr. 23, 1990), 19; Michael Janofsky, "In Drug Fight, Police Now Take to the Highway," *New York Times* (Mar. 5, 1995).

4. Morganthau et al., "Uncivil Liberties?," 19.

5. Linda Greenhouse, "Justices Want Police to Knock in Searches," *New York Times,* wire service, reprinted in *Cleveland Plain Dealer* (June 23, 1995).

6. Loren Siegel, "A War on Drugs or on People?" *Civil Liberties* (ACLU Newsletter) (fall/winter 1989), 1.

7. Ibid.

8. Robert E. Bauman, "Take It Away," *National Review* (Feb. 20, 1995), 34, 35.

9. "Freeze! Your House Is Under Arrest!" *District Line.*

10. Linda Greenhouse, "Court to Weigh 2 Search Cases," *New York Times* (Nov. 29, 1994); Linda Greenhouse, "Justices to Take Up Case on Schools' Drug Testing," *New York Times* (Mar. 29, 1995).

11. Dougherty, "Controversies Regarding Urine Testing," *Journal of Substance Abuse Treatment* 4 (1987): 116.

12. Ibid.

13. Ibid.

14. Vincent Canby, "Cocteau's Skewed View of French Family Life," *New York Times* (Apr. 28, 1995).

15. Jennifer Katleman, "Tucsonan Burned up over Pot Laws," *Tucson (Arizona) Citizen* (Sept. 9, 1994).

16. U.S. Dept. of Justice, *Drugs and Crime Data Fact Sheet: Drug Data Summary* (July 1994), 4.

17. Stephen Witsotsky, "House Hearings on Legislation," prepared statement (Sept. 29, 1988), 10.

18. John Kaplan, *The Hardest Drug* (Chicago: University of Chicago Press, 1983), 107.

19. R. C. Randall, *Marijuana and AIDS: Pot, Politics and PWAs in America* (Washington, D.C.: Galen Press, 1991), 14.
20. David C. Condliffe, "Profile in Cowardice," *Drug Policy Letter* (Spring 1996), 9.
21. George Judson, "Study Finds AIDS Risk in Addicts Drops If Sale of Syringes Is Legal," *New York Times* (Aug. 8, 1995).
22. Maia Szalavitz, "Clean Needles Saved My Life," *New York Times* (June 8, 1996).
23. Joe Peacott, *Disinformation and Distortion: An Anarchist's Expose of AIDS Politics* (Boston: BAAED Press, 1993), 17.
24. Telephone interview, Drug Policy Foundation (Nov. 1996).
25. Joseph Periera, "In a Drug Program Some Kids Turn in Their Own Parents," *Wall Street Journal* (Apr. 20, 1992).
26. Pete Stark, "Not All Drug Lords Are Outlaws," *New York Times* (Aug. 12, 1990).

Chapter 6

1 . R. C. Randall, ed., *Marijuana, Medicine, and the Law* (Washington, D.C.: Galen Press, 1988), 32.
2. Testimony of C. Fred McBee, 1990, cited in R.C. Randall, ed., *Muscle Spasm, Pain and Marijuana Therapy* (Washington, D.C.: Galen Press, 1991), 95.
3. Testimony of Valerie Leigh Cover (1990), cited in Randall, *Marijuana, Medicine, and the Law*, 227–33.
4. Jerome P. Kassirer, M.D., "Federal Foolishness and Marijuana," Editorial, *New England Journal of Medicine* (Jan. 30, 1997), 366.
5. Randall, *Marijuana, Medicine, and the Law*, 175.
6. Tom Brazaitis, "The Illegal Wonder Drug," *Cleveland Plain Dealer* (July 2, 1995).
7. *Marijuana, Medicine, and the Law*, 46.
8. Francis L. Young, reprinted in Randall, *Marijuana, Medicine, and the Law, 2*, 445–46.
9. "Drug Czar Holds Meeting with California Law Enforcement to Discuss New State Medical Marijuana Law," press release (Nov. 14, 1996), Internet weekly news service.
10. Affidavit of G. Fred McBee. Randall, *Muscle Spasm, Pain and Marijuana Therapy* (Washington, D.C.: Galen Press, 1991), 95.

Chapter 7

1. Rob Kincaid, "Freedom Fighter of the Month: Lennice Werth," *High Times* (March 1995), 32.
2. *American Farm Bureau* (July 17, 1996).
3. Article 28 of the Single Convention Treaty on Narcotic Drugs, U.N. 1961, cited in Chris Conrad, *Hemp: Lifeline to the Future* (Los Angeles: Creative Xpressions, 1993), 85.

4. Conrad, *Hemp*, 70.
5. Luigi Castellini, "The Hemp Plant," *CIB Review* (1961–62), 2–31, cited in "Industrial Hemp as a Cash Crop for Colorado Farmers," leaflet (Boulder: Boulder Hemp Initiative Project, 1994), 1.
6. Jack Herer, "Can Pot Save the World?" *High Times Greatest Hits* (New York: St. Martin's, 1991), 128.
7. Stanley E. Manahan, *Environmental Chemistry*, 4th ed., cited in Jack Herer, *The Emperor Wears No Clothes* (Van Nuys, Calif.: HEMP, 1993), 47.
8. Conrad, *Hemp*, 119.
9. Conrad, *Hemp*, 74, 119.
10. "Hope from Hemp," *Yoga Journal* (Jan/Feb. 1995), 12.
11. Senate hearings (July 12, 1937), cited in Conrad, *Hemp*, 37.
12. *Industrial Arts* (May 3, 1937), 131–33, cited in Conrad, *Hemp*, 37.

Chapter 8

1. Charles Strum, "Fall of a Beloved Priest," *New York Times* (Dec. 17, 1991).
2. "School Principal Linked to a Marijuana Ring," *New York Times* (Nov. 1, 1992).
3. The statistics in this section are from U.S. Department of Justice Statistics, *Drugs and Crime Facts, 1993*, pamphlet; "Drugs and Crime Data: Fact Sheet: Drug Data Summary" (July 1994); and *Drugs, Crime, and the Justice System* (Dec. 1992).
4. Marcia R. Chaiken and Bruce D. Johnson, *Characteristics of Different Types of Drug-Involved Offenders*, U.S. Dept. of Justice (Feb. 1988), 3.
5. U.S. Department of Justice, *Drugs and Crime Facts 1995*, 4.
6. Kahler, "Despite Billions Spent in Fight, America Not Saying NO to Drugs," *New York Times* (Aug. 27, 1989).
7. Goldstein, Brownstein, and Ryan, "Drug Related Homicide in New York: 1984 and 1988," *Crime and Delinquency* (Oct. 1992), 459–76.
8. Chaiken and Johnson, *Characteristics*, 3.
9. David Boaz, "The Legalization of Drugs," *Vital Speeches of the Day* (Aug. 15, 1988), 656.
10. Matthew Purdy, "Drug Turf Is Safer as Dealers Avoid Streets," *New York Times* (Jan. 2, 1995).
11. Terry, "Drug Riches of the Capital Luring Poor Youths down a Bloody Path," *New York Times* (Mar. 31, 1989).
12. Mireya Navarro, "Residents Disrupting Drug Trade," *New York Times* (Aug. 30, 1996).
13. Department of Justice, *Drugs and Crime*, 13, 15.
14. Paul Goldstein, "Drugs and Violent Crime," *Pathways to Criminal Violence* N. A. Weiner and M. E. Wolfgang, eds. (Beverly Hills: Sage, 1989), 16–48.
15. Buckley, "Inmate's Viewpoint on Legalized Drugs Carries Ring of Truth," United Press International (Sept. 1985).

16. Ostrowski, "Why Cocaine and Heroin Should Be Decriminalized," Advisory Report of the Committee on Law Reform of the New York County Lawyers Association (April 29, 1989), 30.

17. "Barry, a Political Phoenix, Is Washington Mayor Again," *New York Times* (Jan. 3, 1995).

18. "9 New Orleans Police Officers Are Indicted in U.S. Drug Case," *New York Times* (Dec. 8, 1994).

19. "A DEA Hero Is Busted," *Newsweek* (Aug. 28, 1989), 32.

20. Goldstein, "Drugs and Violence in America," paper (June 16–18, 1993).

Chapter 9

1. Jim Newton, "Privileged Brothers' Lives Shatter in Drug Lab Blast," *Los Angeles Times* (May 20, 1992).

2. Elliott Currie, *Dope and Trouble* (New York: Pantheon, 1991), chapter 14.

3. Ibid.

4. U.S. Dept. of Justice Statistics, *Drugs, Crime, and the Justice System*, (Dec. 1992), 62.

5. Ibid.

6. "Marijuana and Other Cash Crops—1992," report reprinted by NORML.

7. Fox Butterfield, "Prison-Building Binge in California Casts Shadow on Higher Education," *New York Times* (Apr. 12, 1995).

8. Bureau of Prisons, 1995, quoted in "Do You Know Where Your Tax Dollars Are Going," pamphlet (Washington, D.C.: FAMM, 1995).

9. Jim East, "Man's Money Ordered Returned," *Tennessee* (April 23, 1993), 1-B.

10. Robert E. Bauman, "Take It Away," *National Review* (Feb. 20, 1995), 35.

11. Richard Grant, "Drugs in America: Zero Tolerance," *Independent* (June 20, 1993), 14.

12. Ibid.

13. Dale Gieringer, "Economics of Cannabis Legalization," paper, reprinted by Drug Policy Foundation, Washington, D.C. (Dec. 1993).

14. James Sterngold, "Meet Arizona's Happiest Taxpayers," *New York Times* (Oct. 6, 1996).

15. Gieringer, "Economics of Cannabis Legislation," 7.

16. Mathea Falco, *The Making of a Drug-Free America* (New York: Random House, 1994), 92, 102, 180.

17. Sandra Blakeslee, "Crack's Toll among Babies: Joyless View, Even of Toys," *New York Times* (Sept. 17, 1989).

18. Bishop, "Gap Between Cost of Drug Epidemic and State Money Shuts California Clinic," *New York Times* (Feb. 3, 1989).

19. Peter Reuter, "Myanmar's Heroin Habit," *New York Times* (Apr. 1, 1995).

20. Joe Hallinan, "Pot Smokers Find Own Use for High Technology," *Cleveland Plain Dealer* (Sept. 20, 1992).

Chapter 10

1. Barbara Laker and Edward Moran, "Childhood's End: How the Drug Trade Ruins Young Lives," *Philadelphia Daily News* (Sept. 8, 1994).
2. "Study Says 5% of Women Used Drugs While Pregnant," *Cleveland Plain Dealer* (Sept. 13, 1994).
3. Isabel Wilkerson, "Crack's Legacy of Guns and Death Lives On," *New York Times* (Dec. 13, 1994).
4. Laker and Moran, "Childhood's End."
5. "Welfare Roll Study Finds Vast Drug Use," *New York Times* (June 28, 1994).
6. Barbara Laker and Edward Moran, "Drugs Leave a Legacy of Woe," *Philadelphia Daily News* (Sept. 18, 1994), 20.
7. Michael A. Hobbs, "Drug Dealers Feel Money Lure," *Cleveland Plain Dealer* (Feb. 14, 1990).
8. Elliott Currie, *Dope and Trouble* (New York: Pantheon Books, 1991), 89.
9. Joseph B. Treaster, "In Brooklyn, Young Love Is Crushed by the Anguish of Crack and Heroin," *New York Times* (Oct. 21, 1990).
10. Elliott Currie,. *Reckoning: Drugs, the Cities, the American Future* (New York: Hill and Wang, 1993), 141.
11. "Job Program Participants: Still Poor and in Need of Assistance," *New York Times* (Apr. 10, 1995), 12.
12. Currie, *Dope and Trouble*, xvii.
13. Currie, *Reckoning,* 11.

Chapter 11

1. Nathaniel C. Nash, "On the Drug Battlefields of Bolivia, U.S. Sows Dollars and Reaps Hate," *New York Times* (Mar. 13, 1994).
2. Tim Golden, "Violent Drug Trafficking in Mexico Abounds," *New York Times* (Mar. 8, 1993).
3. Tim Golden, "Mexico's Drug Fight Lagging," *New York Times* (Aug. 7, 1994).
4. Quoted in Jorge Pinto, letter to the editor, *New York Times* (Aug. 7, 1995). Pinto is the consul general of Mexico.
5. Golden, "Mexico's Drug Fight Lagging."
6. Larry Margasak, "Heroin Ring May Be Shut Down after 34 Arrested Worldwide," Associated Press (Oct. 12, 1996).
7. Hsein Chou Liu, *The Development of a Single Convention on Narcotic Drugs* (Bangkok: Academy of New Society, 1979), 3, 16.
8. Theodore Vallance, *Prohibition's Second Failure* (Westport, Conn.: Praeger, 1993), 97.
9. Golden, "Mexico's Drug Fight Lagging."

10. U.S. Dept. of Justice, Drug Enforcement Administration, *United States International Drug Control Activities Report* (1988), 11.

11. Michael Specter, "Opium Finds Its Silk Road in Chaos of Central Asia," *New York Times* (May 2, 1995).

12. James Brooke, "Cocaine's Reality, by García Márquez," *New York Times* (Mar. 11, 1995).

13. Specter, "Opium Finds Its Silk Road in Chaos of Central Asia."

14. Linda Greenhouse, "Justices Back Property Searches of Foreigners in Foreign Nations," *New York Times* (Mar. 1, 1990).

15. James Brooke, "Peruvian Farmers Razing Rain Forest to Sow Drug Crops," *New York Times* (Aug. 13, 1989).

16. Christopher Torchia, "Colombian Peasants Protest Destruction of Coca Plants," *New York Times* (Aug. 25, 1996).

17. Nash, "On the Drug Battlefields of Bolivia."

18. Pete Hamill, "The Great American Drug Muddle," *Lears* (Mar. 1990), 159.

19. Quoted in Stephen Klinger, "Pro-Drug Ruling in Germany Stirs the Pot and the Politics," *New York Times* (Mar. 3, 1992).

20. James Brooke, "Colombia Reimposes Curbs on Marijuana and Cocaine," *New York Times* (June 2, 1994).

21. Philip Shenon, "Singapore Executes a Dutch Engineer Arrested on Drug Charges," *New York Times* (Sept. 24, 1994).

22. Nicholas D. Kristof, "China Metes Out Death at Drug Rally," *New York Times* (Oct. 27, 1991).

Chapter 12

1. John P. Smith and Peter Gorman, "Holy Smoke: Civil Disobedience and Compassion Fuel Our Church," *High Times* (Sept. 1994), 32–33; Peter Gorman, "Marijuana Church Founder Gets 121 Months," *High Times* (June 1995), 34–35.

2. *Atlanta Journal* (Aug. 22, 1993).

3. Shay Totten, "Hemp Fans Spread Word—and Seed," *Burlington (Vermont) Free Press* (May 15, 1993).

4. Quoted in "Gingrich on Drug Dealers," *New York Times* (July 15, 1995).

5. Timothy Leary, lecture, University of Colorado at Boulder (October 1994).

6. Stephen Gaskin, personal interview (March 1995).

7. Michael Janofsky, "Baltimore Grapples with the Idea of Legalizing Drugs," *New York Times* (Apr. 20, 1995).

8. Steven Wishnia, "Election Roundup," *High Times* (Mar. 1995), 32.

9. *Official State of Washington Hemp Voter's Guide*, pamphlet, Washington Citizens for Hemp Reform (1996).

10. U.S. Department of Justice, *Drugs and Crime Facts* (1988), 31.

11. "89% Say Yes," *ACT News* (Summer 1994); *Parade* (June 12, 1994).

12. Drug Policy Foundation Survey, 1990, cited in J. Marshall, "Results of Drug Pro-hibitions' Repeal Praised," *California Lawyer* (Sept. 1994), 98.

13. Tom Mealy, "Fallout from Marijuana Vote Drifts Down to Starks," *Lewiston (Maine) Sun-Journal* (Mar. 18, 1992).

14. David Fitch, "Battle Begins on Home Marijuana Use," *Anchorage Times* (July 15, 1990).

15. Ron Kampia, "Should You Take the Initiative?" *High Times* (Mar. 1995), 60.

Chapter 13

1. "Why Do People Use Illicit Drugs?" *Drugs, Crime, and the Justice System*, 20.

2. Kirk Kidwell, "The War on Drugs," *New Americans* (Nov. 7, 1988), 32.

3. Cirrhosis death rates for men went from 29.5 per 100,000 in 1911 to 10.7 in 1929; admissions to state mental hospitals for alcoholic psychosis declined from 10.1 per 100,000 in 1919 to 4.7 in 1928; Mark H. Moore, "Actually, Prohibition Was a Success," *New York Times* (Oct. 16, 1989).

4. Cited in Arnold Trebach and Charles Rangel's statements in congressional hear-ings in September 1988.

5. 1993 High School Senior Survey, reported in U.S. Dept. of Justice, "Fact Sheet: Drug Data Summary" (July 1994), 4.

6. Philip J. Hilts, "Lawmaker Applies Pressure for Regulation of Nicotine," *New York Times* (Aug. 1, 1995).

7. Ethan Nadelmann, "Switzerland's Heroin Experiment," *National Review* (July 10, 1995), 46–47.

8. John Kaplan, *The Hardest Drug: Heroin and Public Policy*, (Chicago: Universi-ty of Chicago Press, 1983).

9. Carter, "Keep Costs of Illegal Drug Use in Perspective," *Wall Street Journal* (Aug. 14, 1989). About 55 million Americans smoke; 85 percent say they would like to quit; 61 percent have tried to quit and failed.

10. National Household Survey on Drug Abuse, 1992, U.S. Department of Health and Human Services, cited in Falco, 24.

11. Julio Martinez, director of New York State Services of Substance Abuse, con-gressional hearings, Sept. 1988.

12. Dr. Herbert D. Kleber estimates that legalizing cocaine would produce 20 mil-lion addicts, quoted in Joseph A. Califano Jr., "It's Drugs, Stupid," *New York Times Magazine* (Jan. 29, 1995), 40.

13. Tom Morganthau and Mark Miller, "Hour by Hour Crack," *Newsweek* (Nov. 28, 1988), 77.

14. Quoted in David S. Martin, "Legalization Called Option in Drug Fight," *Penn-sylvania Patriot* (April 10, 1991).

15. Eddy Englesman, quoted in "Permissive Drug Policy Keeps Lid On," *Cleveland Plain Dealer* (Dec. 10, 1993).

Glossary

addict: a person dependent on drugs

biomass: organic matter, such as plants, that can be converted to fuel and used as an energy source

cannabis: Latin classification for the plant that produces marijuana, hashish, and hemp fiber

Cannabis indica: variety of cannabis known as "skunk," which can grow anywhere in the world

Cannabis sativa: variety of cannabis known for its high THC content; grows in warm, tropical climates

contraband: illegal goods

Controlled Substance Act (CSA): the comprehensive federal plan for controlling drugs that are believed to be dangerous and subject to misuse

convention: treaty or agreement

decriminalization: when violation of a law is treated as a civil instead of a criminal offense

de facto legalization: when a law is not enforced

drug abuser: a person who uses drugs to his or her detriment

drug addict: a person who is dependent on drugs

drug cartel: an organization of drug traffickers

drug control policy: the various ways a government goes about controlling the drug problem

drug czar: director of the federal drug policy agency

Drug Enforcement Agency (DEA): federal agency charged with controlling illicit drug trafficking

drug testing: testing a person's urine, hair, or blood to detect use of an illicit substance; in random drug testing, tests are performed without advance warning

eradication: destruction of illegally grown drug crops

extradition: surrendering a suspect to another jurisdiction or country for prosecution

hemp: a commmon name for cannabis; cannabis used for industrial purposes, e.g. hemp fiber and hemp paper. Jute and other tropical plants also produce fiber known as "hemp"

interdiction: seizing drugs in transit or upon arrival at a country's border

intravenous drug user (IDU): someone who injects a drug like heroin by needle into a vein

legalization: repeal of laws against recreational drug use

mandatory minimum sentencing: requiring a judge to impose a sentence of incarceration (prison, jail, or other confinement) for a specified term for certain categories of offenders. Under mandatory minimum sentencing there is no option of parole or suspension of a sentence

Marinol: a drug made of synthetic THC, the cannabinoid in marijuana that causes euphoria and also helps reduce vomiting and nausea

methanol: fuel that comes from plants, such as corn, soybeans, sugarcane, and other sources of biomass

money laundering: funneling cash profits from illegal drug sales into legitimate bank accounts, businesses, and other operations

mules: people who smuggle drugs across a border by carrying them

posse: term used to describe members of certain gangs

probation: a crime sentence where the person remains at liberty but is subject to conditions and restrictions, such as limits on travel or required drug testing and treatment

sinsemilla: female cannabis plant that is unfertilized with pollen from the male plant; known for its high THC content

THC: Tetrahydrocannabinal, the psychoactive component in marijuana

three-strikes-and-you're-out: mandated life sentencing without parole for those convicted of a third violent crime or serious drug crime

For More Information

Bugliosi, Vincent T. *The Phoenix Solution: Getting Serious about Winning America's Drug War*. Beverly Hills: Dove, 1996.

Conrad, Chris. *Hemp: Lifeline to the Future*. Los Angeles: Creative Xpressions, 1993.

Currie, Elliott. *Reckoning: Drugs, the Cities, the American Future*. New York: Hill and Wang, 1993.

Falco, Mathea. *The Making of a Drug-Free America*. New York: Random House, 1994.

Herer, Jack. *The Emperor Wears No Clothes*. Van Nuys, Calif.: HEMP, 1993.

Musto, David F. *The American Disease: Origins of Narcotic Control*. New York: Oxford University Press, 1987.

Randall, R. C., ed. *Marijuana, Medicine, and the Law*. Washington, D.C.: Galen, 1988.

Stares, Paul. *Global Habit*. Washington, D.C.: Brookings Institute, 1996.

Internet Resources

Families Against Mandatory Minimums (FAMM)
http://www.famm.org/

National Clearinghouse for Alcohol & Drug Information
http://www.health.org/

National Organization for Reform of Marijuana Laws
http://www.normal.org/

Monitoring the Future Study Data
http://www.isr.umich.edu/scr/mtr

U.S. Sentencing Project
http://www.sproject.com/

Index